Black Crusoe, White Friday

BLACK CRUSOE, WHITE FRIDAY

Memoirs of 'Paddy-Ali', Irish Eccentric

by

Paddy Monaghan

SATELLITE BOOKS: London

First published 1979 by Satellite Books (Publishers)
Kendall House, 9 Kendall Road, Isleworth
Middlesex

© Paddy Monaghan and Satellite Books (Publishers), 1979

ISBN 0 905186621

World Rights Reserved

Made and printed in Great Britain by
The Garden City Press Limited
London and Letchworth

Illustrations

between pages 60 and 61

TOP LEFT Paddy the boxer. He introduced boxing to Abingdon. i
RIGHT In Muhammad Ali's London Hotel during Paddy's first meeting with the champ.

BOTTOM Muhammad and Paddy during the early stages of their friendship. The Champ is reading some of the fan letters from the *Ali Fan Club*, of which Paddy is the president.

TOP Paddy accompanying Muhammad at a business meeting in New York. ii
MIDDLE One of the many chat-shows during which Muhammad Ali introduced Paddy to the audience.
BOTTOM Together in Miami, U.S.A. . . . *Black Crusoe, White Friday*.

TOP LEFT Muhammad playing with Paddy's kids. iii
TOP RIGHT Muhammad with Paddy's family in the author's house. Fourth from left is Paddy's mother.
BOTTOM Paddy and Muhammad Ali outside the Champ's home in Philadelphia, holding *The People's Champion* trophy presented by Paddy on behalf of the fan club.

"Paddy-Ali" with his drawing predicting the outcome of the second Ali-Frazier showdown. iv

TOP Muhammad at play. His brother Rahaman looks on right. Paddy is third from left on the porch. The place is in Northern Ireland, where Ali fought Al Blue Lewis. v
BOTTOM Fearsome heavyweight boxer George Foreman (on the back of a motorcycle) seconds before his confrontation with Paddy, whose *Ali is our Champ* banner is visible in the background.

Paddy's wife Sandra with their children – all rabid fans of Muhammad Ali. vi

TOP Paddy dining in New York with the family of legendary ex-boxing champion Jack Dempsey. vii
BOTTOM The crowd that mobbed Muhammad outside Paddy's home.

TOP Muhammad Ali with Paddy shaking hands with local Morris Dancers outside Paddy's home. viii
BOTTOM Muhammad Ali with Paddy addressing an impatient crowd outside Paddy's home.

For my mother and father

Chapter One

To say that my story begins on the evening of April 28th, 1967, when the TV newscaster announced the ignominious boot of Muhammad Ali from his throne, would fall short of the region of accuracy. It begins long before then, as far back as February 19th, 1944, when a small farming village called Ederney, in Northern Ireland's County Fermanagh, experienced my arrival into the world.

I was the youngest of six, evening the score for my parents with three boys and three girls. The best parents in the world, mine were – Mum everything a mother should be: loving and gentle and all, you know; and the old man – well, he was a character, I suppose; but to me he's the greatest. Once he could have boasted about never having to work under anyone for a living, what with the wealth-bag his parents left him in their will. The 'Monaghans-of-the-Mill', as my ancestors were known, had a long history as well-to-do owners of many acres of land and property in the environs of Ederney, but all that changed when the old man's parents passed on when he was just ten years old. Three years later it was his guardian aunt's turn to move on, leaving Dad alone in the world to wade his way through the mine of wealth his parents had left him. He soon eloped from his college in Dublin and, reassured by the bulge of cash in his pockets, sought the carefree life, which he was well into by his mid-teens. To manage on his own at such an early age proved to be no problem in itself: his problem was generosity and naivety, surpassed by a craze for gambling, all of which contributed to holing both his pockets.

In the end Dad, last of the Monaghans, was booted out into the cold by his bank manager, and found himself working for one of the farm labourers who had worked for him at one time! But to this very day he's something of a legend to the old-timers back there in Ederney, and I'm proud of him.

The family joined him in England when I was a toddling three-year-old, and we eked out a wretched existence in just one room here in Abingdon. It's a very Conservative town, Abingdon, situated six miles outside Oxford, with too many reserved and weak-minded people in it. Now that Mum and Dad are retired, one ambition that constantly gnaws my innermost is to make up to them for the heartbreaking hardships that they both sowed to reap our family survival. If only my performance in boxing had rivalled my obsession, I would have acquired the wealth to allow my parents some very deserving pleasures. Unfortunately it hasn't worked out the way I want.

As far back as my memory can stretch, I've always wanted to box. I never had the chance as a kid or teenager because there was no boxing club in Abingdon. As a five-year-old, while my chums took to the *Beano*, *Dandy* and similar comics, Mum was already placing my weekly orders for boxing papers and magazines. My inherent inspiration to be a fighter must have triggered off my reputation as a rough-tough kid. This reputation followed me up to secondary school, and had damaging effects on my tuition. In fact, I spent more time at school shovelling dung, toiling on the school garden in the summer, and assisting the caretaker scooping coal than I spent with the teachers. *Paddy Monaghan* was forever singled

8

out to assist when work became copious for the gardener or caretaker, and all in all I spent more time using the shovel than using a pen.

By the time I left school at the age of fifteen, I could barely read or write. My first job was digging trenches and laying cables for an electrical installation company. Dad then suggested I become an electrician and to apply for an apprenticeship. I did so – only to be turned down owing to my inability to read and write. My gifts lay exclusively in the art of fighting, it seemed. At the time Abingdon was described by the press as the roughest town in England. It was the regular scene of mass gang-fights and bar-room rough-and-tumbles, mainly against paratroopers stationed at the local RAF camp. With the reputation of a formidable street-brawler, the name Paddy Monaghan had a parrot-like repeating effect on the townsfolk. My ego and manhood certainly enjoyed a life of glory, but my pocket suffered: I was a regular visitor to court, and consequently an equally regular contributor to the court funds with the fines I forked out. On one particular occasion, however, at the age of sixteen, the sentence was to a detention centre for walloping a bouncer – 'Big Jumbo' they called him – at a Saturday night dance. The world was terrified of the guy. He antagonised my resentment of bullying when he flattened some arm-in-a-sling weakling who happened to get in his way. Several pals tried to hold me back when I made my way towards Big Jumbo; they were pleading, terrified that the guy would pulverise me. Sure, the guy dwarfed me, but what did I care: in a moment of passion, who yields to reason? I ignored their exhortations, and threw myself at the 'gorilla'. God knows how many punches I threw or where I threw them: what I best remember was his great hulk hitting the dirt like a sack of wet cement – there to lie in oblivion, his face a mask of blood and bruises. Sure, I became the hero of the town for that feat, but the cops didn't think so. Big Jumbo had pressed charges, and on the night of the day that I flattened him, the cops came to my house to arrest me. Three months at the detention centre I got, while Big Jumbo got a police escort out of Abingdon, never to be seen or heard of again, even though his folks still live here.

Yeah, I was a case; but I never did anything to be ashamed of, you know – just the crazy punch-ups and motoring offences. Although I am no longer a practising Catholic, I was brought up to obey the ten commandments; but, well . . . no commandment said thou shalt not fight or drive a car without a licence, did it?

I said cheerio to the boisterous life around the age of twenty. You've got to hand it to my wife Sandra – she did the trick. Her beauty and the subsequent romance that blossomed between us inevitably closed my mind to almost everything in life except herself. She was a quarter Chinese, Sandra was, with the unmistakable Oriental surname of Chung; her old man was the son of a First World War Chinese interpreter who married an Abingdon girl.

Sandra's parents almost hit the roof when they heard that their gently-reared daughter was going steady with the likes of Paddy Monaghan, and could have got high blood pressure with their efforts to keep us apart: they confined Sandra indoors in the evenings, but we still dated in secret. We met every lunch hour, and sometimes took days off work to spend riding the buses in Oxford just to be together. After a time, it just had to happen, you know: I plucked up courage and marched boldly to her home to assure her parents that as far as Sandra was concerned, I had the most honourable of intentions. They had their doubts, but you couldn't blame them. Anyway, they both realised that Sandra and I were in love – and I was to prove just how honourable my intentions were when I asked her to marry me. Oh was she over the moon! We had a short engagement, and on May 8th, 1965, our hands were joined in holy matrimony. Would you believe that the whole town turned out to witness the occasion as if they had to see it to believe it. Word was to reach us that cynics were all predicting the number of *months* the marriage would last. My attitude was a mental 'V' sign to the lot of them. They've had no choice but to eat their words – because till this day, fourteen years later, Sandra and I are still happily married, and blessed with five beautiful children – one boy and four girls.

I've long since abandoned the boisterous life, thanks to Sandra, but I suppose I do suffer a touch of nostalgia when I cast my mind back to those good old spirited days. My initial interest in boxing will always remain with me like a roaring fire. I have to admit, when I look back to those years before I met Sandra, years of near-poverty and wretched existence, I recognise that it was the fight game which kept me above sanity level. Otherwise I fancy I would have been just like so many millions of people who had experienced the same sort of background as I had – living on the extreme edge, ignorant of the world beyond my immediate surroundings, no real interest to find out, you know – just more or less hanging around waiting for death. But thank God, violence was my saviour, my merciful outlet from the world of wretched anonymity which fate had deemed for me. Thank God, I was gifted with curiosity comparable to the north-seeking nose of a compass – always eager for something new and out of the ordinary. It was in the fight game that this something manifested itself, and was for me like manna from heaven. This manifestation has had a devastating impact on my life, and will, I fancy, influence my life for the rest of my days.

The manifestation came in the form of a human being, a man, of a hue that people call black, a human being who is, in my eyes, the nearest creature on earth to a god. I first set eyes

11

on this man one Saturday afternoon in July 1962 on television. His *raison d'être* was boxing, and I had followed his progress in the boxing magazines since he became a professional in 1960. He was a tall man, beautifully muscled, boyishly handsome, with a honey-coloured complexion and a skin as unblemished as any I had ever seen. To a stranger, he would have passed as a model, even as a sweet 'mother's boy', and any suggestion that he could be tough enough to join the punishing world of professional pugilism would have been laughed out into orbit by our conjectured stranger. Yet he was the best example of a true pugilist that nature had offered since before the dawn of time. When I saw him for the first time on telly that afternoon, and witnessed in fascination his unique and inimitable execution of Lord Queensberry's noble art, I knew that I had to find out more about him. From that day onwards, I was to devote a great chunk of my life to the man. Outside of my immediate family, he has been my *raison d'être*. It doesn't sound real, does it? But that's how it has been.

I remember that Saturday afternoon way back in 1962 as though it were yesterday. "Yes," I said to myself, "this guy's going to make it big."

I sifted through innumerable literature about him and was proudly aware that he and I had a few things in common: we were both from oppressed ethnic groups, both experiencing an underprivileged upbringing, seeking an outlet from misery with our fists, with a genuine love for the art of boxing. I memorised so much information about his past that within a very short time I became a self-appointed authority on the man. Like the millions of fans that came to love him, I craved for the occasion of saying hello in person. But I was one of those 'semi-existent half-humans' – or so class had decreed – who could only *dream* of the privilege of meeting famous people. So the first stages of my close relationship with Muhammad Ali were conducted in the world of dreams, and I was prepared to make do with that. You have to play the game the way the cards fall.

When the Louisville Lips began to blast self-praise and the world was agitating in vain and mounting frustration for a well-placed blow to effect the permanent buttoning, my love for the man reached its hilt. He suited me perfectly, for my curious nature was easily titillated by the extraordinary; what was more, the sport for which I virtually lived was being bestowed with some colour and extra vitality by this man. For once the world began to show real interest in boxing.

It came as no surprise to me when he stunned the world by defeating the fearsome Sonny Liston in his first world championship fight: it had long become my conviction that there was nobody alive who could beat Muhammad. It was naturally a delight to have been one of the very few people in the world who predicted a victory for Muhammad. Because of my love for him, I felt I was the happiest person on earth after his victory. This happiness, I well remember, was faintly tainted by a sense of sadness brought about by a vain yearning to get to know him as a person and to be his personal friend. But that seemed only possible in the world of fantasy.

I was a firm believer in every individual's right to his own views and beliefs, providing that his outlook does not interfere with the rights of others. So when Muhammad began to express his devotion to the Black Muslim religion, announcing the change of his name from Cassius Clay to Muhammad Ali, I was all behind him, especially as I felt that he and his race had good cause for their convictions. Therefore when Muhammad was stripped of his title for the reason of his religious beliefs, the effect this had on me personally can never be adequately conveyed with words. I had never been a person of words, not having had the privilege of proper

13

education and articulate speech: besides, I've always believed that words are women and deeds are men. Although I was over three thousand miles away from Muhammad when he came to grief, it made no difference to me: I felt strongly enough about it to be motivated into positive action, come what may.

Even in the dream-world in which I habitually pictured myself as Muhammad's faithful companion, I could never have truly envisaged that the action on which I embarked in my quest for justice would reward me with a real-life friendship with Muhammad. That, indeed, was what happened. In my case, therefore, fact has become even stranger than fiction. It became a friendship which I have come to regard as a symbolic parallel to that between Robinson Crusoe and his man Friday. But this time Crusoe is blessed with black skin and Friday with white.

Yet what I did to come into this windfall was, to me, the easiest thing in the world: anybody could have done it. But I suppose I saw it as a gracious act of providence that it should be I of all people who happened to make the first move. Only very recently did a friend point out that what I did was, in a sense, one of the most difficult actions to embark on − if only for the very significant reason of eccentricity. Eccentricity, I gather, is a 'characteristic' that not many people possess (or would want to possess, I recognise). So only an eccentric person, or something of an idiot, would have carried out my form of protest. Well, all I can say is that I thank God for this eccentricity, if that's what it was, because the rewards it has brought me were, again, luxuries that most members of my underprivileged clan could only dream about.

It was after dinner on the 28th April, 1967, the day I heard the news of Muhammad's misfortune, that I marched out of my council home, a writing pad in one hand, a biro in the other, calling on the homes of neighbours and friends. Some

sympathetic, others indifferent, the general attitude was that
a protest from Paddy Monaghan, labourer inconsequential,
was about as likely to change the minds of the world boxing
authorities as a bishop electing to run the Mafia. Nevertheless, if it would make me happy, they would write their
signatures and addresses.

Thereafter, in the week that followed, the route of protest
took me to pubs, shops, hotels and housing estates in Abingdon and Oxford – the end of which brought in a large amount
of support in the form of signatures from both sexes, from
the young and the not so young. Alas – when the local papers
flashed the news that Paddy was taking on the World Boxing
Association, it sparked off speculation that this was just a
passing phase. But as time progressed, people became more
puzzled when they discovered how wrong they were. Why
should anyone want to devote his time to trying to solve the
problems of a man living three thousand miles away across
the Atlantic? they wondered – a man whom he doesn't even
know, has never met, and most probably never would meet,
for the mere reason of this man's unique boxing talent and
showmanship? Was this a mere search for personal glory?

Time has proved that there was no quest on my part for
personal glory. At that time only my parents and Sandra
knew how strongly I felt about justice for Muhammad. I had
been given the nickname 'Paddy-Ali' by the townfolk, but
this appellation merely denoted a boxing-craze sort of liking
for Muhammad, as far as my pals were concerned. They
weren't to know that my feelings about Muhammad went far
deeper than that. The night I first heard the news about his
misfortune, I truly experienced a strange sensation within
me, like some inner voice notifying me that I had been
chosen to stir up support for Muhammad. You can laugh at it
if you want, I wouldn't blame you – I recognise that it
sounds a bit far-fetched, but that is the truth. The night I

15

heard the news, I had moved restlessly around the sitting-room till late, touching this, touching that, trying to let the rage flow out of my fingers.

Be that as it may, by the end of August 1967, the signatures and addresses had exceeded over a thousand – a sizeable number of which came from several rallies and one-man demos I held in London, with my cause displayed on the banner which I had designed – *ALI IS OUR CHAMP*. News of my campaign circulated by word of mouth – evident by the letters of support from people all over Britain stating that they had been informed about it. This support received a massive boost by the publication of some of my persistent letters of appeal in boxing journals, and by October 1967 I was boasting 8,004 signatures and addresses. By then I had sent off several batches to the World Boxing Association in Phoenix, Arizona, accompanied by a letter written in the strongest possible language protesting against their so-called justice. The patronising nonsense I received from the then executive secretary, Mr Jay Edson, said how good it was to hear from people such as myself, since it showed that boxing can boast of such a rabid fan. This reply was not only infuriating, but it convinced me that the only way to impress it upon these authorities that I was not just some frustrated rebellious nut striving for attention was to press on with my campaign and raise a staggering number of supporters. The figure I had in mind was something in the region of twenty thousand.

Though my campaign took up the greater part of my life, I did find time to devote to my passion, boxing. But even this I now performed more as a tribute to Muhammad than to the sport in its own right. It was the magic of Muhammad, in the early stages of his professional career, that caused me to introduce boxing to Abingdon. With the help of a friend, I converted a local disused railway station into a gym and in 1968 formed the Abingdon Town Amateur Club. In due course I found better premises in an old disused church, forming, also, a committee, and calling on local contacts to use influence to obtain old punch bags, old gloves, skipping ropes and other boxing requirements. It took eighteen months of hard work to get the boxing club running the way I wanted it, with the encouraging number of forty-two members. Having got the whole thing going, I had no desire to head or join the committee myself: my interest lay in the boxing side of the club. I yielded to the temptation to have a go and see what my own fists could produce. Alas – it was not as easy to put it together inside the ring as outside: I found that out the hard way, and a couple of years later hung up the gloves, having won twenty-three out of thirty-four fights at welterweight division. I realised with regret that I had nothing like the experience I would have liked to have at my age, and that to reach championship stage the aspiring boxer should don the gloves between ten to fifteen years of age. I should reveal, however, that in truth I was very keen to continue boxing. I was obliged to retire on medical grounds. My doctor informed the boxing officials of a certain illness I had (which I would rather not reveal), and on my request the officials allowed me to offer a different reason to the folks for my retirement. So only my wife and my parents were aware of the real reason. There was a lot of local surprise and disbelief when it was learnt that I was packing up boxing, and the local papers made a big thing out of it. It was good to be regarded as the local favourite, you know; it broke my heart when I felt I was letting everybody down.

So my campaign on Muhammad's behalf grew more intense. My banner became a routine sight in Abingdon, Oxford, Trafalgar Square and Speakers' Corner. Letters of support from kids, pensioners, mums, gentry and working men continued a steady flow into my home from all over the world, some from countries I had never even heard of before. By mid-1970, the signatures were nearing their twenty thousand mark.

At that period in time, Muhammad and I had one thing very strongly in common – we were both suffering in more ways than one. On his side, the plumber who carried out repairs in his Philadelphia house was disconcerted to be given a cheque that bounced, and when he confronted Muhammad, was told, "No bread, man." While Muhammad's lawyers battled on in vain to retrieve his precious boxing licence, some people suggested an alternative – that he follow in the footsteps of his white-woman-loving predecessor Jack Johnson by jumping bail and fleeing to another country. But Muhammad's integrity and pride were impenetrable. So his lawyers tried to obtain permission for him to fight abroad, which not only failed, but served as a reminder to the Government to revoke his passport – just in case . . . So suffer Muhammad and his wife had to, with the Black Muslims paying just about enough to feed them for his lectures at their different mosques.

In my part of the world, the happy atmosphere that the birth of my daughter Saydee brought to our home yielded to the misfortune of Sandra developing breast fever. She was hospitalised for two weeks, but thank God made an amazing recovery in the course of the few months that followed. Then fate struck a hard blow with my own illness. It was the same one which had forced my retirement from boxing, and had plagued me for a long time. Now it had grown steadily worse. The family doctor was called to my home and I was taken to The Churchill Hospital in Oxford, where I underwent a week of rigorous tests for further sightings of my illness. The tests were carried out under the expertise of Professor Richie Russell, to whom I am eternally grateful for all his care and concern. He was the same doctor who broke the news that my boxing days were over. He was now to reveal that the results of my tests indicated conclusively that I had to relinquish my job at the M.G. car factory, where I had worked for the past four years. Before that the only kind of job in which I had displayed any ability was a hod-carrier, and that, said the professor, was out of the question. I had to face up to the fact that my working days were virtually over, and I recall that my initial sentiment as I lay in the hospital was one of acute depression, nearing something of despair. I had always been an independent type of person; but now here I was a victim of circumstances over which I had absolutely no control. It was hard to come to terms with the idea that I would now have to rely on state handouts as the sole means of my family's survival. Nevertheless, as time progressed, I learned to live with my illness, but the constant awareness that state handouts are the breadwinner in my home gnaws my pride till this day. I had never realised the importance of independence until fate took it away from me.

By the time I was dismissed from hospital, I realised that I could not dwell in an eternal world of depression, and what helped me to pull through more than anything else was my love for my family, and, I suppose, for Muhammad Ali. I realised I had to do something to keep my mind active, and was thankful to recognise that the numerous letters that continued to pour in from all over the world in support of my *ALI IS OUR CHAMP* campaign guaranteed a busy life ahead.

So there lay the marauding situation for Muhammad and I – Black Crusoe and his white Man Friday, both trapped on a desert-island of unemployment and misfortune. To preserve my sanity, I continued my campaign more relentlessly than ever, and found ultimately that I had over-reached the total number of names and addresses for which I had aimed. I had collected single-handedly the overall total of 22,224.

Though the boxing authorities in Arizona failed to reply after I sent off the last batch of signatures to them, I remain convinced that a petition containing 22,224 names and addresses made them don their thinking caps: a few months later, on September 14th, 1970, Muhammad was given back his boxing licence. Such was my jubilation that I recognised that my depression in hospital at the prospect of life-time unemployment was something I could just look back on as a bad memory. The great man had risen again, and somehow this made the future seem bright. I know that had it not been for my campaign I might well have ended up a pathetic human cabbage whose *raison d'être* was simply to await an appointment with death. I recall thinking about the unusual circumstances that had occurred at the end of my three and a half years' campaign for Muhammad: now that Black Crusoe was leaving that dreaded desert-island on which we were both suffering, I, Man Friday, was still stranded on that island. But I did not mind. All that I cared for was his freedom, even if I died with my efforts to free him.

But thank God I was still alive to enjoy the colourful years that were to come with that freedom.

Chapter Two

Muhammad defied all the so-called experts' speculation that ring-rust had set in and eroded his old boxing magic by soundly thrashing the 'Great White Hope' Jerry Quarry in three spectacular rounds. The old magic had not died: it had merely been wrapped away like treasure in a secret safe.

However, the flag-waving Uncle Sams who were craving for Muhammad's defeat found their glory on March 8th, 1971, when Muhammad lost the decision against Joe Frazier, who had become champion during Muhammad's exile. I saw the fight on closed-circuit television in London in an atmosphere charged with a thousand volts of electrical excitement, deafened from time to time with the hysterical chants of 'Alee, Alee' as the two men pounded out the issue that had been styled 'Fight of the Century'. As I waited at the end for Muhammad's hands to be raised, I went into a paralysed daze when the ref announced Frazier as conqueror. I couldn't believe it. Frazier had fought like a tank, certainly; but there should have been no doubt in anyone's mind that Muhammad had done enough to win, despite the knockdown he suffered in the last round. The angry conclusion I reached was that this had been a political decision – planned to heal the injury to Uncle Sam's pride.

I wrote to all the newspapers to express the feeling that

Muhammad may not be champion as far as the US boxing authorities were concerned, but certainly he was *The People's Champion*, calling on readers to join a fan-club that I had decided to start for our champ. I deprived my dwindling bank account of £45 to pay for the printing of Muhammad Ali calendars and postage costs, which I despatched to fans who answered my correspondence in the boxing journal. As I did not know Muhammad's address in the States, I proposed to hold on to his fan-mail until his next visit to England, when, hopefully, I could hand them to him in person.

In the meantime, I had read about Muhammad's manager, Herbert Muhammad, visiting England, and hurried to his London hotel to introduce myself. I gave him a poem I had composed about Muhammad and asked if he would be good enough to hand it to the great man. The poem was entitled *TRIBUTE TO THE PEOPLE'S CHAMP*, and read thus:

In the past we have seen some outstanding champs;
They learned a lot of skill in the training camps;
But we've never seen skill performed so naturally
Until we saw the great Muhammad Ali.
The Rock, Joe Louis and Jack Dempsey were pride of the
*   nation*
And they were well respected by their generation.
But if we live to be a hundred, we never would see
Anyone to equal Muhammad Ali.
The Boxing Authorities acted like fools,
When they decided to change the Queensberry Rules.
It was a very foul blow by the WBA
That finally took his title away.
There is one point I would like to make clear:
Our Champ's entitled to his beliefs, and has proved to be
*   sincere.*

22

Black Crusoe, White Friday

It was all because he said 'no' to Uncle Sam,
But so did millions opposed to the war in Vietnam.
Ali only had two fights in almost four years,
And when he was matched with Frazier I didn't have any
fears.
Ali won the fight as far as I could see
And I reckon the judges should be charged with robbery.
Although I must admit he overplayed and overclowned,
And was put down by a left hook in the final round.
Ali will win the return I really am convinced,
And Frazier's claim to the title will definitely be rinsed.
Ali is the greatest ever – of that I have no doubt:
And I've studied them all inside out.
Although we've never met, to me he's like a brother,
Because the respect I have for him can be equalled by none
other.
There is one ambition that is left for me:
It is to shake the hand of the great Muhammad Ali.

It was one Friday morning in May, not long after I met
Muhammad's manager, that a letter arrived from Philadelphia, USA, addressed simply to 'Paddy'. Sandra was clean-
ing out the sitting-room as I opened it, thinking it was
another fan-letter. I recall brightly the great wallop that my
heart gave against my chest when I saw at the top of the
letter-page the words *MEMO FROM MUHAMMAD ALI.*

The letter was in long-hand and was brief.

Thank you for your beautiful poem. Keep up the good work. I
will see you when I'm in England. Good luck.

I recall that after being initially confounded, I showed the
letter to Sandra. Happiness sent tears trickling down her
cheeks like morning dew down the petals of a lily.

Be that as it may, I was inundated with letters in response to the Ali–Frazier fight, and it is a significant fact that the vast majority of the letter-writers were unimpressed by the opinions of the so-called experts who considered Frazier a convincing winner. This, together with my strange sense of loyalty for Muhammad, instilled in me more than ever the resolution to get the fan-club underway. It dawned on me that the only means available to me and the one sure method of achieving success was to resume my one-man vaudeville that had effectively won support for my original campaign for Muhammad. I knew that the majority of world public opinion still regarded Muhammad as the true champion. I had adopted for him the title of *THE PEOPLE'S CHAMP-ION*. I recognised that no one would be expected to tell Joe Frazier that! Yet I realised that if ever this opportunity arose, I would expect it of myself to express public opinion on behalf of Muhammad and those millions who had supported him and my campaigning in the past. As fate would have it, that opportunity (and responsibility) did arrive when Joe Frazier visited London on June 14th, 1971. He was accompanied by his pop-group *THE KNOCKOUTS* – an appropriate name to describe the manner in which most of his ring opponents had faced defeat. I and my *ALI IS OUR CHAMP* banner were at the terminal building at London Airport to confront him, totally ignored by the number of pressmen present. But it was not ignored by Joe Frazier when he emerged from Customs with his group, looking immaculate, I must confess, in a stark white suit, black-laced shirt, and dark glasses. It was the first time I had seen him in person – some six feet of solid ebony muscle and broad-shouldered, dwarfing my five-feet-seven 'tot'. He was truly the toughest and most powerful-looking man I had ever seen. His pugilistic face somehow accentuated his 'human tank' appearance – the expression popularly used to describe his relentlessness in the ring. Nevertheless, this was the moment for truth. After taking a huge breath, I stepped forward and blocked his entrance through the Customs door with my banner raised high. He stopped open-jawed, as though refusing to believe my courage. Next moment he raised out one hand to halt his entourage then slid his bag across the terminal floor. He then took off his glasses and put them in his pocket. His eyes narrowed. A sudden blanket of silence covered the terminal as everybody took in the scene: it was as if the whole world was suddenly frozen in one moment of time.

Frazier broke the silence.

"Put it down!" he snarled.

"No I won't," I said, and held the banner as high as possible, my heart-beats quickening with every second. I hollered, "You can't fool the world, Frazier. I'm here to tell you that you're only the newspapers' champ. We're the real experts, and you and we know that Muhammad beat you."

His eyes ignited fire. He bent his massive frame and pressed his forehead against mine, and repeated furiously, "I said put it down you fucking little bastard!"

"No I won't!" I answered defiantly, "you don't scare me."

Whereupon I felt the pressure on my forehead increase as he started to push me backwards with his forehead. He was issuing threats of violence if I did not accede to his order, decorating his threats with obscenities loud enough for everybody to hear. He continued shoving and I shoved back, still keeping the banner high, verbally giving as good as I got. I stared fearlessly into the pools of fury his eyes swirled.

Next moment we were pulled apart by members of his pop-group. As they tried to restrain him, the only time I lowered the banner was when a member of his group kicked out and caught me on the leg. I tried to set him up for a right-hander when I was jumped on and ushered from the building by two policemen. As I was leaving, Frazier, who was still being restrained, yelled after me, "I wish I could get you in the ring instead of Ali. I could take care of you."

He was on ITN News that evening, interviewed by reporter Michael Oliver, who had been at the airport to escort Frazier to the TV room and had witnessed the incident. When Oliver mentioned the confrontation, Frazier suggested flippantly that I was part of some big organisation who had planned it after losing money on the fight. Some organisation – one man!

When Michael Oliver telephoned me, I told him the correct facts of the matter and he expressed deep regret not to have had TV cameras on the scene. He was amazed at my courage and said that he had to see it to believe it. Frazier had evidently told Michael Oliver that I had come 'close to death' and probably would have reached it had he not been restrained.

I was pleased with my 'demo', if only because it had earned publicity for my campaign, you know: certainly old Joe Frazier and the so-called experts got the message.

On Muhammad' scene, the Champ's loss against Frazier seemed to have earned him even more respect all over the world – I suppose because of the graciousness with which he accepted the officials' decision. In no way did it affect the showmanship, the sense of humour, the poetry, and the flapping of the Louisville Lip! On June 28th, 1971, he scored the greatest knockout of his career against the vindictive politicians who had robbed him of his title and boxing licence. Now the Supreme Court voted 8–0 in Ali's favour. This was an achievement that made him more contented than with any ring victory – a win against that very exclusive club which rules the country called 'The Establishment', and by a points score that no boxing authorities had ever given him – eight–nil.

Now with the Frazier fight over and those legal worries relegated to the dustbin, Muhammad stepped into the ring again on July 26th, and with usual colour, scored a spectacular triumph over his former sparring partner Jimmy Ellis – the first of a series of fights he proposed to have in preparation for his return duel with Joe Frazier.

It was on the morning of October 11th that he popped into London for an 'Ovaltine' promotional tour. Quivering inside with excitement, I was one of a large crowd at the airport terminal building to welcome him. I had, in my possession, a bag containing thousands of world-wide fan-letters sent in to me for Muhammad *and* a long red carpet that was to welcome his gracious dancing feet. The atmosphere as the crowd waited was thick with awe and intrigue – enough to set the hairs on a dog rising. It was almost as if the presence of some entity from the unknown were imminent. The magic of Muhammad was at work even before he was seen.

Sheer determination forced me through the crowd to be nearest the Customs entrance to present my welcome, the noose of excitement strangling me. Minutes later he was strutting coolly towards me, smiling and greeting all and sundry, boasting no great entourage – just a middle-aged slack-jowled white man who looked like a business counsellor. As a commotion swept through the crowd, I crossed the barrier and spread out the red carpet.

From the mists of memory I recall his voice booming, "Hello there everybody", and the crowd returning the greeting. But such was my awe that I cannot recollect what wit he cracked, on seeing the carpet, that sent an explosion of laughter through the crowd. He gave a cursory glance at the young man at the other end, not knowing then who I was, then stepped on the carpet and approached – to tumultuous applause from the crowd.

The moment he reached my end, I offered my hand, saying, "Hello Champ, I'm Paddy Monaghan."

At once his face blazed with remembrance. "So you're Paddy Monaghan?" he exclaimed, shaking my hand vigorously. "I've heard that you're ma main man."

His greeting then took on the form of an embrace and hearty backclaps as he expressed his happiness to see me. By now the police were trying to control the crowd, who had surrounded us and were threatening to crush the great man to death with their love. Here was Muhammad Ali in front of them in living colour, dressy, huge, a fine specimen of a man, with a baby face that raised the question why on earth he chose fighting as his career and not filming.

"C'mon, Paddy," he said, "you're comin' to ma hotel with me. We got a lot to talk about."

I followed him into the VIP lounge, where he gave an exhilarating press conference, most of which was spent hollering with typical modesty that he was going to spank Joe Frazier in their next encounter like a stern papa would thrash a wayward son.

Later, as I, Paddy Monaghan, unemployed labourer, sat with Muhammad Ali and his companion in the back seat of the chauffeur-driven Rolls-Royce smoothly humming its way towards West London's Lancaster Hotel, it was as if I was sitting on a cloud of dreams. It seemed too incredible to be true. This was something I could never have believed possible during those years of campaigning. Strangely enough, overawed as I was by the circumstances, I was not conscious of any feeling of nervousness. There was the inevitable thrill of travelling in a Rolls-Royce for the first time, intensified of course whenever Muhammad took his attention off his companion to talk to me; but I was not nervous. This was probably because of the warm friendliness of his personality and the fact that his voice was not the loudspeaker I had expected: it was a gentle, low and serene contralto, making me feel as if, amid my excitement, I was in a strange and wonderful world of calmness. I felt both at ease and aghast. During that short car-ride, I felt as though I had known Muhammad for a long time; yet we had known each other only twenty minutes.

There were many people who visited his hotel suite while I was there to pay him their greetings. Between these visits he would turn his attention to me and we would talk about some of my efforts over the years. He had heard 'just talk' about those efforts, he said. "But you really been doin' all those things they say, Paddy?" he asked.

There was no doubting that he fully appreciated the extent of my sincerity and devotion to my campaign. As a clear gesture of his appreciation, he surprised me by writing down the times he expected to be back in London from his visits to various parts of England to promote Ovaltine, saying I should telephone him at the hotel to arrange another meeting. I was surprised because I had expected that this golden opportunity of meeting the great man would be the first and last, despite the extent of my efforts. I reckoned that somebody generally regarded as the most famous man in the world would give me a polite kind of brush off. But I soon dismissed that thought.

Later when I was leaving his suite to return to Abingdon, he asked me to assure the writers of the fan-mails that he would read all their letters personally whenever he could get the chance.

On that visit he was in England three days and I met him twice more, having telephoned him at the times he had nominated. He honoured me with a free ticket to the Royal Albert Hall, where he rounded the evening's professional boxing with exhibitions.

Just to have seen the guy in living colour would, quite

29

honestly, have been good enough for me. To have shaken his hands was even better; and to have ridden in the same Rolls-Royce, treated to a snack in his suite, and invited to the Albert Hall, was more than I could have bargained for. So what words then could I, or indeed, the combined literary efforts of Shakespeare and Dickens, possibly find to describe my feelings when, on the last occasion I saw him in his suite, he wrote down his home telephone number in the States, told me to ring him in three weeks and reverse the charges, and we would discuss plans for me to visit the States as his guest?

Nor could words describe the astonishment among my pals in Abingdon, many of whom thought that I had taken up a course in (pardon the expression) bullshitting. But they were left in no doubt when I spoke to Muhammad a few weeks later on the transatlantic phone. He told me that my BOAC flight-ticket, which he had paid for, would be waiting for me at the check-in lounge at London Airport on the day of my departure, when I would be bound for the States. My feelings at the time are beyond description.

I had never even been on an aeroplane before, and, like Muhammad, nursed a fear of flying. I recall that as the Super VC10 jetliner sped down the runway and swung into the sky that fog-enveloped morning of February 17th, 1972, I experienced once again that blazing awareness that this was a treat that underprivileged non-entities like myself could relish only in impossible dreams. We all know to believe in fact and not fiction. Yet I recognised that sometimes people become more convinced by the story of a dream than they do with reality. An encounter on the plane during the flight confirmed this. My seating-partners were a friendly American couple. They immediately introduced themselves to me barely after they were seated, and presently we embarked on a casual conversation. I did not mind answering their somewhat nosey questions about my home, my family, my unemployment, etc. Then, with about a couple of hours left before touch-down, they couldn't resist asking me how I could afford to visit the States if I was unemployed. I replied casually, "Oh, I've been invited over by Muhammad Ali personally as his guest."

The expressions on their faces after that information told all. First they exchanged glances, then frowned, cast quaint smiles at me, and said, "Oh really . . . heh-heh!" Clearly a nut, they thought. And for the duration of the flight, all I got from them was the occasional quaint smile and heh-heh!

Chapter Three

The plane touched down in Philadelphia late in the afternoon to weather that made the cold we had left behind in London seem a warm blessing.

After clearing Customs, the announcement of my name on the intercom directed me to one of the ticket-desks, where I was given a cordial welcome by a broad-smiling black man with a husky voice and handshake so powerful I could feel it in my boots. He introduced himself as an employee of Muhammad's and regretted that the Champ was unable to be here to meet me himself, for he had been called away at the last minute to Pittsburg on business.

The drive in Muhammad's limousine was made enjoyable by this man's interest and amazement at my campaign on behalf of Muhammad back in lill-ol-England. "Yeah, Ali's been talking a lot 'bout bringing you over here," he said.

After about an hour's ride, we were in suburban Cherry Hill, New Jersey, where Muhammad was living at that time, and the limousine swung into a picturesque tree-lined avenue of cool, exquisite-looking homes laid neatly behind well-cultivated lawns and hedgerows. Muhammad's home was a large cream-coloured Spanish-styled villa, elegantly surrounded with corrugated iron railings. Set against a background of forest-like trees, it boasted a three-car garage, a large blue mobile home-bus, and a vintage Oldsmobile.

I was welcomed by his former wife Belinda and by his mother, who was there helping Belinda to look after her three kids, as a fourth child was due the following month. The facial resemblance between Muhammad and his mother was striking. She was a sweet, gentle lady who spoke with obvious love and pride about her two sons Muhammad and Rahman.

Being a person of aesthetic disposition, I could not resist marvelling and expressing wonder to Belinda and her mother-in-law at the splendour of the home. I had never been amid such elegance before. The home was decorated in magnificent taste, with the beauty of antiques and soft colours. Every wall in the living-room boasted a large book-case, whose titles were obscured by the wrought-iron and glass doors. In one corner was a huge beautifully-styled piano, and Muhammad's mother explained with some amusement that such was her son's passion for music that he often employed a lady pianist to bang away at the keyboards for him once a week. There was an elaborate sound system in the room, and his mama said that he was a fan of both classical and pop music. His craze for classical art was also evident by the sculptures and oil paintings that graced the walls and flat surfaces. The back-windows looked out at the garden, and Muhammad's rectangular swimming-pool was surrounded by an imitation lawn, beyond which lay the woods.

While Belinda prepared a meal in the kitchen, Muhammad's mama coped with her three grandchildren in the living-room and joked about her boy's wild ways during childhood, showing the gold teeth that replaced the original which he had knocked out while she tended him in his crib.

After a succulent meal, Belinda dropped me off at a nearby hotel, as Muhammad had instructed; he had booked me in

Black Crusoe, White Friday

before setting off for Pittsburgh, leaving a message to the effect that he would collect me the following day. Until that occasion, I had never been in a hotel before, except when I visited Muhammad in London. The room was grand, fitted with a colour television and a bedside telephone, etc. But my mind felt too exhausted to dwell on the thought of Paddy Monaghan being treated to such unaccustomed luxury, and I went straight to bed – to be immediately engulfed by sleep.

It was the loud shrill of the telephone that jerked me awake at about eight o'clock the next morning. Semiconsciously I reached over and picked up the receiver. "Hullo there, Paddy," said the voice, "this is your friend Muhammad Ali."

The last clouds of sleep were instantly dispersed from my head. We engaged in a fairly lengthy conversation, and he said he had rung several times during the night but got no reply, guessing correctly that I had been out like a log. He had come all the way from Pittsburgh to pick me up, he said, and was speaking from his home. We were to go back to Pittsburgh that same morning, because he was contracted to box several exhibition bouts while on tour of America. He had decided to take me with him and show me round the States. He told me to be ready and he would pick me up from the hotel lobby in twenty minutes. I was over the moon.

He arrived punctually in a huge black Cadillac, and as usual was in high spirits, his greetings entailing the bulging of eyes that had become a popular aspect of his showmanship. Being a passenger in his car as we drove to the airport was quite an experience, if only because he was the fastest driver I had ever sat next to. He had a passion for cars and for fast driving, and this was to cause us some embarrassment in due course.

*   *   *

35

Black Crusoe, White Friday

By the end of my first two weeks in the USA, we had travelled many thousands of miles together and shared luxurious surroundings and experiences. To him these were no doubt as common as eating, drinking and sleeping, but to me it was all so different from the life to which I was accustomed in a small Oxfordshire town. It all seemed so unreal when I reflected on my circumstances. Here I was in America, a personal guest of the great Muhammad Ali, sometimes helping him out in his corner during exhibition bouts, travelling all over America with him in planes and Rolls-Royces . . ., and soon I would be back in Abingdon, thumbing a lift to London to watch him box on closed-circuit television. Life really didn't make sense sometimes.

Like many other raconteurs of thrilling experiences, I am faced with the nail-biting question where exactly to start – and take the unusual decision to start from the very end, from Muhammad's candid parting words as we said farewell: "Paddy, always remember, little brother, that you are my friend." Yes, a few simple words – but words which, to me, were the highlight of those two weeks and I knew he meant it.

I had come to realise just how amazing the guy really was. There was something extra special about him in his response to ordinary working-class people, and, equally, in their response to him. Everywhere we went, his itinerary in each big city would consist of personal appearances at plush banquets, etc. But he also had his own personal itinerary in each big city, in that whenever possible he would visit the ghettos and mix with the junkies, drunks and drop-outs, looking into their glaring eyes, and chiding gently, "Kick the habit, brother." After accompanying Muhammad on such occasions, I recognised that although the 'haves' at those plush banquets appreciated his appearances, the 'have-nots' in the ghettos clearly appreciated him more. Ironically, it was those visits to the ghettos that impressed me most of all. The sort of receptions that he was accorded at the places we visited was an experience of a lifetime to witness at first hand. I thought back to the television news scenes I had seen in the past of the tumultous welcomes bestowed on some great world leaders during public appearances. I acknowledged that the people who flocked out to wave and cheer did so purely out of reverence and for the experience of seeing them in person. I thought, too, of the hysteria that possessed pop-fans during festivals given by the Rolling Stones or concerts by Elvis Presley, Tom Jones, etc., recognising that it was caused not so much by the personalities of the pop-musicians as by the magic of their music, their singing and the well-rehearsed seductive motions of their dancing. But with Muhammad, it was just personality that hypnotised the crowds. There was an enthusiasm and joy in the reception he got from the crowds which were in a class of their own – unrivalled by that shown to any other celebrity in the world. Today, in fact, possibly throughout recorded history, only the reception given to The Messiah which the biblical stories ask us to imagine can one say positively was above that shown to Muhammad. It was not just the screaming and mass-hysteria that illustrated the depth of the people's love for him: it was more-so the facial expressions of the masses as they gaped at him that told all. To illustrate this, he and I were driving in suburban Philadelphia on one occasion, and he stopped outside a children's primary school. "I wanna say howdy to the kids, Paddy," he told me.

We clambered out and he led the way to one of the class-room doors, which he casually opened, poked in his head, and declared coolly, "Ahhmm looking for trouble."

I well recall the pandemonium that prevailed. Within a very short time the entire school had spilled out-side – pupils, teachers and the headmaster. There was the

37

inevitable vociferous clamour as the young pupils crowded around him, trying to touch, striving to attract his attention. The great man raised his hand and ordered authoritatively, "Now then everybody, you got to control yourselves; ah don't want none of you getting hurt." Abruptly a devastating hush fell. He shook hands with all the amazed teachers, picked up and cuddled some of the children, instructing them all to work hard, for education was the most important necessity in life. It was fascinating to behold the expressions on the faces of teachers and pupils: they were chiefly one of bliss, as if their love for Muhammad was beyond fulfilment. My chief regret is not to have had a camera with me.

Muhammad and I made similar surprise visits to other children's school, and the same look of ecstasy would flame on the kids' faces. If it was not a school or the ghettos, it would be some road-sweeper or newsvendor who would receive his attention: impulsively Muhammad would stop his Rolls-Royce, get out and stroll over to engage them in conversation. It was always a delight to witness the people's disbelief at Muhammad's abrupt materialisation – disbelief, too, that a person of Muhammad's status should care to treat people so individually. I acknowledged once that had the President of the USA or his opposing candidates made a similar sudden appearance to any of these individuals, it would *not* be done as a consideration for their welfare – as they would like us to believe – but for the sole reason of drumming up votes for election times. That reminds me – I recall how sullen-faced and tight-lipped was actor-turned-politician Ronald Regan of California when the crowds completely ignored him as they chanted 'Alee . . . Alee . . .'. This happened back in July 1972 when we entered the Gresham Hotel in O'Connel Street, Dublin. The only people near Governor Regan were his confused bodyguards, employed to keep ordinary individuals well away when it is

not election time: inevitably members of the public become
cautious and suspicious when approached by politicians. But
with Muhammad Ali, they felt no inhibition whatsoever, for
he would chat and joke with them as if of the same class and
wave-length – a clear invitation to them to feel free to communicate with him as they wished. This they always did.

I was so unaware of the fact that this great man was so
outstandingly extra-special outside the boxing ring. Though
I did so in my heart, I never thought of openly commending
him for the sincerity and thoughtfulness he displayed
towards people individually, if only because he had given me
his reasons in just five words three days after my arrival. He
and I were speeding along the motorway in his sleek Lam-
borghini sports car to see his business agents in Philadelphia.
The weather was below freezing point and snow was pelting
down. Presently Muhammad noticed a sailor unsuccessfully
thumbing a lift in the bleak weather. He slowed down and
stopped. The sailor ran up in obvious relief, and when he saw
just who the good Samaritan was, exclaimed "My God! I
don't believe it!" – and fell back in somewhat the fearful
ecstasy of a dog interviewing his first jumping toad. His
astonishment caused Muhammad to laugh. The Champ got
out to let him get into the back seat.

As we started off again, Muhammad asked the guy where
he was heading. The sailor said Virginia. Muhammad asked
him how he could possibly want to hitch-hike in a weather
like this. The sailor stammered that he couldn't afford the
fare.

When we arrived in Philadelphia, Muhammad drove to
the airport – where he further confounded the sailor by
slapping a number of dollar notes in his hand, saying,
"C'mon, ah'm gonna put you on a bus for Virginia."

This was the first display of his generosity that I witnessed
in the States, and I was touched to the point of feeling aghast.

After he had seen the sailor off and returned to his car, there was silence for a while as I mulled over in mind whether or not he may think it corny if I broke into compliments. I felt him glance at me. Either the expression on my face must have betrayed my thoughts or he was a mind-reader. He said quietly, "Consideration hurts no one, Paddy."

I expressed agreement, adding that it was a pity few people shared the same attitude.

The people's immediate reaction to Muhammad left me in little doubt that he was instantly recognised by individuals who would merely gape at the most celebrated actor, royalty, politician or statesman. There was never an occasion, be it in his car, in the streets, in the air, name it – where his materialisation did not provoke admiring comments, the drop of jaws, the bulge of eyes, the pointing of fingers, the autograph requests, the handshakes, the adulations. Muhammad, in turn, never failed to acknowledge these. On one occasion, an elderly outspoken fan announced, "Ah never used to like you, Champ, 'cause the newspapers influenced me not to. But now that ah've met you ah know that the press gave me the wrong impression."

Muhammad, appreciating the old man's honesty, replied, "Sometimes it's best to read between the lines."

I acknowledged that not many men could be capable of such remarkable display of energy in travelling such as Muhammad was gifted with. There was the constant pressure for him to be here and there, particularly the business commitments and public appearances, which, of course, meant lack of sleep; but it was clear that he had adapted himself to such exhausting requirements. On a couple of occasions I awoke in the morning to find him gone to meet some businessmen, and no sooner had he returned than he was ready to pick me up and set off again to another part of the States.

Black Crusoe, White Friday

Of all the places we visited, Oklahoma City stands out in my mind. The people we met all over America were delightful, but the reception Muhammad and I had in Oklahoma was the most tumultuous of all. A massive crowd was at the airport on our arrival. We got into an enormous limousine, at the wheel of which was a chauffeur ready to follow a large motor-cycle escort. Presently the motor-cade led us through the city to our hotel. The streets were lined tight with what must have been the entire population. The people had turned out with cheers and 'Welcome' banners to greet Muhammad. Their cheers could even be heard above the non-stop screeching of deafening welcome blasts of car horns in – and out – of sight. Even these were drowned by the crowd's chanting of 'Alee . . . Alee . . . Alee . . .'.

Clearly Muhammad meant more to the people than a mere celebrity or World Heavyweight Champion, I recognised. There is no doubting that he is the greatest human symbol of the public's respect, love and admiration, and their crescendos are proof that he has reached deep into the hearts of the people. People need Muhammad, not the World Heavyweight Boxing Championship. The world needs him because he is 'The People's Champion'. He would indeed create a tremendous and delightful impact in history as President of the USA. He can contribute more to world peace than any present-day politician or statesman, because his policies are for justice, freedom, equality and peace. His characteristics mirror the support of world public opinion for his policies, and in so doing, with the combination of the people's love, respect and admiration, achieve something which no other political leader in history has ever achieved on a global scale.

If Muhammad ever decided to become a candidate for the Presidency, I am convinced that he would win. To some people this may sound like humorous fantasy. But who would have believed twenty years ago that Ronald Reagan, just a 'B' movie actor at the time, would become State Governor one day? More important, who, years ago, would have suggested that unknown peanut farmer Jimmy Carter would be inaugurated as President in 1977? Although Muhammad had never indicated to me any desire to enter politics, I continuously reflect on how logical it would be for a man of his great status to become President. It is not as though he is inexperienced in the behaviour of politicians: he was, after all, stripped of his title in 1967 – the victim of political injustice.

One would have thought that the awesome crowd-pulling potential which Muhammad has would necessitate an army of bodyguards around him to act as a barrier. The nearest he has to a bodyguard is one Chicago cop who accompanies him from time to time. He is a black character called Pat Patterson whose hefty build and tough no-nonsense expression would stand him out in any rugby team. Yet underneath the tough-guy appearance, Pat reveals a peace-loving individual and a warm friendly personality, with great consideration when dealing with hysterical fans. He appreciates that the fans have nursed their love for Muhammad for an eternity, so consequently when presented with the great man himself before their eyes in living colour, pressure inevitably builds up. Pat then has to move in to prevent the Champ from being crushed to death with love. I have seen him in his working role on many instances, but only on big official occasions like tours and big fights when large excited crowds assemble does he move in, using discretion more than muscle to guard his revered master.

Talking about cops, Muhammad and I were caught up with 'The Speed Cops' in America several times. Though Muhammad is something of a perfectionist inside the boxing ring, he fell somewhat short of that category when it came to

42

observing the rules of speeding, consequently setting
motor-cycle cops on our heels with sirens whining for him to
stop. Muhammad would jokingly feign worry to me as he
slowed down, saying, "Gee Paddy, what we gon' do
now? – we both done for." Then, after we halted, the cop
would head towards us. Always the firm expression on the
face of every cop changed to amazement on recognising the
unmistakable offender. Muhammad would look at me with a
mischievous grin and a wink. Then he'd say to the cop,
"Hallo, officer, that sure is a nice motor-cycle you've got
there; and pretty powerful, too. I noticed you were going
pretty fast back there; what speed can it reach flat out?"

The frustrated and confused cop would tell Muhammad
about his motor-cycle, then, as if he almost forgot – "But
. . . but, Champ, you were speeding!"

"Oh was I? Gee – ah never realised how smart your
uniforms were until now. Y'see, ah don't think ah've ever
met a speed cop before. Look at that uniform, Paddy, smart
ain't it?"

I would play along, saying, "Yeah, Muhammad, that's
really cool."

Muhammad would continue, "Paddy's a friend of mine;
he lives in England. Man, that sure is a fine motor-cycle
you've got there."

Again the cop would remind him, "Champ you were
speeding."

"Yeah," retorted Muhammad, "that motor-cycle is a nice
colour; it matches your sharp uniform just right."

By this time the cop would usually be won over, and end
up asking Muhammad for autographs for all his family.
Normally the cops reminded Muhammad about their duty to
uphold the law, making a courteous request that he should
observe the speed limit in future.

Muhammad's boyish charm did not always work in such a

43

situation. I was with him on a couple of occasions where there was no room for favouritism, and he was handed speed-violation tickets. In fact, he told me that he had collected quite a few in his time.

*   *   *

Privileges followed privileges during my times with Muhammad. Perhaps one of the more memorable occasions was the night of my twenty-eighth birthday when we went to New York together and I mentioned casually that I would like to see Broadway. He took me along, and we enjoyed a spectacular show. Little did I know at the time that he was supposed to be in Oklahoma City that same day. I found out only the following day when we arrived in Oklahoma and read local press statements about Muhammad arriving a day later than expected 'because of an important business meeting'.

While in Oklahoma, he decided to buy me three top-quality suits, two pairs of slacks, five shirts and three pairs of shoes – all as a present. I well remember that this generosity caused me to stay awake late into the night reflecting with deep gratitude on the tremendous hospitality that this lovely human being had showered over me. I had never met anyone in my life who had shown me such consideration, and sometimes I still found it hard to come to terms with the idea that this was all happening to me.

On several occasions I worked in his corner for exhibition bouts, sprinkling his face with cold water in between rounds and giving him a sip of water to drink; and after each bout he would get hold of the microphone and entertain the large audiences with wit and poetry, promising unfailingly to destroy Joe Frazier in their next encounter. He would then introduce me into the ring, telling the audience about "ma friend Paddy Monaghan from Abingdon, England", giving a glowing testimonial about my efforts over the years on his behalf – including my airport showdown with Joe Frazier. He would then hand *me* the microphone to have my say. The first time this happened – in Pittsburgh – I well recall that the gulp which went down my throat felt like a small boulder. It was heard by Muhammad, who could not resist laughing. Paddy Monaghan addressing a distinguished audience not only seemed the joke of the week (since I had never spoken to an audience before), but more unlikely than science fiction. I couldn't believe it at first. But once I got going, I felt fine, and even managed to throw in a bit of good humour – to tremendous applause. On one occasion, I told a packed audience about Muhammad, "If friendship means having to die for someone, then I would be ready to die for Muhammad at any time." The applause to this was thunderous. Muhammad knew I meant it, and responded with a simple nod and a smile as the audience clapped and roared.

After the speeches, people would even clamour to get my autograph, and those I gave out must have been sufficient in number to decorate the walls of a small living-room. I remember the first time this happened as I stood beside Muhammad handing out signatures. Jokingly he chuckled, "Paddy you're famous now." I just could not understand why all those people wanted my autograph, and I recall thinking "If only the folks at home could see me now, then they would have to believe it!" I knew that if I told them what had happened, they would just laugh me off as crazy, convinced that my imagination had got the better of me.

Then there were the occasions that Muhammad took me

with him to college and high-school campuses where he lectured, and to lavish dinner banquests held in his honour and attended by some of the most prominent people in the land. Always – no matter what the occasion – he would introduce me to the audiences, each time handing me the microphone for a few brief words of hello. Likewise at press conferences and on television and radio . . . consequently there I was, good old inconsequential Paddy, shaking hands with famous celebrities, politicians, and US citizens. One particular function stands out in my mind. It was at a birthday party in honour of the famous comedian Jackie Gleason, held at a millionaires' haven called The Inverary Golf Club House, in Miami. A sudden hush was followed by the deafening cheer as Muhammad made his entrance. We were shown to our seats at the dinner table. Muhammad was seated on my right next to the actor Mickey Rooney. Barely had we sat down than Muhammad introduced me to his host and the other guests; and in the course of the meal I was engaged in conversation with Mickey Rooney. At one point of our chat, he said, "Welcome to millionaires unanimous," then enquired, "and what line of business are you in, Paddy?" I answered, "I am a penniless and unemployed builders' labourer." Rooney laughed, genuinely believing I was pulling his leg.

"Yeah? And how come you are now among the cream of America'a High Society?" he quipped. "Ha, ha, now c'mon Paddy, be serious, what line of business are you in?"

I tried to assure him that I was being serious. "Would you believe that the day before I came to America I even had to borrow the money from my mother to get a haircut, and arrived here in a shirt I borrowed from my brother?"

By now Rooney was bouncing with laughter, and presently, said, "Gee, you're good fun, Paddy, What gets me is how can you look so serious when you're joking."

All I could do was smile and shrug impotently. I remember just sitting back to look at the cream of America's High Society which surrounded me, listening to their descriptions of the various views which could be seen from their high penthouses, all the while aware that reality for me was on the ground floor.

Late the same night, back in our hotel suite, I lay in bed amid the sweltering Miami heat, thinking over the memories of the last two weeks in America. Although I had savoured every second of what felt like being in a different world, what always impressed me most was Muhammad himself. He was nothing like the anti-white image the press critics claimed he was. Clearly he was not the sort of man to have hate in his heart.

It was about 2 a.m. when I looked in the darkness towards the bed opposite and whispered, "Muhammad, are you awake?"

He repeated a couple of loud snores and replied humourously, "No, man, ah'm fast asleep."

With that he switched on the bedside lamp, sat up and readjusted his pillow, then reached over and poured himself a glass of water from the container on his bedside table. "Ah, that's better," he mumbled, then asked, "What's the matter, Paddy, can't you sleep?"

I told him no, explaining that the heat was all new and strange to me in the month of February. He suggested that I should drink plenty of water, because it prevents dehydration in hot climates. "In the Persian Gulf," he added, "doctors advise people to drink no less than eight pints of water each day."

He laughed, and I quipped, "Cor blimey, I'd be pissing on the rug if I was in Persia."

Soon we were involved deep in conversation, and this ultimately led me to bringing up the subject which puzzled

47

me somewhat. I queried, "Why do the press critics keep trying to put you down, Muhammad?"

He answered, "Ah donno why, Paddy, and ah don't really care about newspapers, 'cause the public are more intelligent than the press seem to realise. Ah guess it's just because ah don't say the things that the newspapers and the establishment want me to say, and ah don't do the things they want me to do; but that don't bother me none, 'cause ah know that people of today have learned through past experience to read between the lines. They don't need any little old cigar-smokin' reporter or fat-assed editor telling them how to think; the people know that it makes more sense sometimes to read between the lines."

I nodded in full agreement, then asked, "Why does the press state that because of your religious beliefs, you regard the white race as devils? I know it isn't true, but why do they print those things?"

He shook his head, and replied, "No, Paddy, ah hates no one, and all Muslims are taught not to hate. Ah know that some newspapers have printed such lies and rubbish in their feeble attempts to distort the facts, but only the ignorant accept those reports seriously, and words from an ignorant man impress no one. When we Muslims talk about the white devils, it is just a representative term we use as a simplified example to describe those white slave masters who murdered, raped, butchered and robbed our black ancestors of their identity, freedom, justice and equality for four hundred years. The black folk over here are still living in a limbo as a result, 'cause if a man don't know his name and he don't know his true identity, then he may just as well be dead. Yeah, Paddy, those white slave masters could never be described as saints, so now you understand who we were talking about when we referred to the term 'White Devils'; but we don't live with hate in our hearts or vengeance. We don't want revenge, 'cause today's generation are not to be blamed for their ancestor's actions four hundred years ago."

Again I was in complete accordance. I always found during my conversations with Muhammad a feeling of complete mutual understanding. It was as though we were on the same wave-length. Though he was much more intelligent than I was, I could still communicate freely with him. There was no need for acting or pretending: we could just be ourselves whatever the mood. I always felt at ease with Muhammad, and as time was to prove I now regard him as the only true friend I've got.

After our lengthy conversation in the hotel that night, I remember saying to him, "Muhammad, I'm with you all the way."

He replied, "Paddy, you're ma man; you're talking like a brother. Ah knows you're with me, and we'll always be with each other all the way just like brothers. When you says something, ah knows you mean it, and from now on you are ma brother."

I regarded this as an honour, and said, "I mean it too."

We went on talking, and he expressed his regret for not having displayed much academic prowess. It occurred to me, though I didn't say so to him, that there was really little cause for him to feel regret, seeing as he had acquired for himself all the knowledge that school did not give him. With other great boxing champions in history, the road from success had taken them to the good life – gambling, drink, night-clubs and women. That, as far as they were concerned, was the be-all and end-all in life. But Muhammad was different: here was somebody who had made a spontaneous effort to find out something about the world he lived in – and had thoroughly succeeded . . . evident by the mere fact that he should be constantly invited to give lectures at colleges and universities all over the world: such invitations are not usually bestowed on self-educated individuals.

One diversion that our conversation in Miami that night took was to my own circumstances – my past and present efforts on his behalf, my future prospects. "Paddy," he said, "you've proved your loyalty to me in the past, now you must think about the future, and when you get back to London find yourself a good job with a good income. You won't have to work half as hard as you're doing now, and they'll pay you for it. You takin' too much of a gamble to continue as you have done, and ah don't want to see you end up broke . . ." (He never knew it, but I already was broke!) . . . "because ah'm so heavily committed already, and ah can't afford to subsidise you if things don't work out for you."

"I'm no fucking parasite, Muhammad," I told him, shifting my sitting position on the bed to look squarely at him; "I'm no hanger-on. All the hanger-ons won't crawl out from under their rocks until you regain your championship, and as far as I'm concerned, you don't need the championship. I'll never come to you with any hard-luck stories and beg for money."

"You're a real brother, Paddy," was his reply, "ah knows you mean it."

It was some years ago since that conversation took place, and Muhammad – if he recalls it – would still be in no doubt about my sincerity, because till this day I've never asked him for a penny or gone to him with any hard-luck stories: and I never will.

When the time came for my return to Britain, he drove me to Miami Airport himself. On arrival, he wrote down a list of telephone numbers where he could be contacted in the next few weeks, and handed it to me, saying I could call him any time I wanted to and reverse the charge-call. Then he dipped his hand into his pocket and pulled out two hundred-dollar bills. As he passed them to me, I stood back shaking my head, and said, "No, Muhammad, you don't have to do that with me."

He replied, "Ah knows that, Paddy, but it'll just make me feel better if you take it; now here."

With these words, he shoved the two hundred dollars into the top pocket of my jacket. He then placed both his mighty hands on my shoulders as he said, "Don't forget, Paddy, ah think of you as a true friend. Always remember that. We are brothers."

As the big bird revved its engines and took off into the night sky, I remember looking out of the window down at Miami's panoramic sprinkling of colourful lights with a lump in my throat.

I whispered, "So long, brother."

Chapter Four

From the glorious weather and luxurious surroundings of
Miami, it was back to the dreary cold English winter and to
my home in the ghettos of Abingdon. It was also back to
trouble, which first hit me at Customs at Heathrow Airport.
I was obliged to fork out most of the two hundred dollars
from Muhammad so that I could keep the new clothes he
had bought me. I had never been to an airport before until
Muhammad invited me to the States, so was completely in
the dark about the Customs procedure. Consequently I
walked into the 'Nothing to Declare' section, and of course it
was just my luck to be picked from random for a baggage
search. Inevitably they saw the new clothes with the price-
tags still attached, and there was duty payable for these. So it
was farewell to most of the two hundred dollars I had to my
name.

But worse was to come. Back home in Abingdon the
authorities welcomed my return by stopping my social security payments in the belief that *I* had paid for my trip to
America myself. I put up a vociferous protest, assuring them
that it was Muhammad Ali who had invited me over to the
States as his personal guest and had paid for the trip and all
other expenses. But this fell on sceptical ears. The old Charlie interviewing me laughed insincerely saying, "That's the

best one I've heard!" He then told me to wait. I sat there waiting for hours, during which time I noticed the staff at the office frequently pointing me out and sniggering. Ultimately my name was called out and I entered one of the cubicles for another interview. It was the same old Charlie again.

He came direct to the point. "Do you really expect us to believe what you said in this statement?"

"Yes," I answered, "it's the truth."

"Well, I'm sorry we cannot accept this, and therefore you will get no unemployment benefit. Good-day."

With this he got up and walked away, leaving me furious and frustrated.

To them it seemed to defy all logic that Muhammad Ali, the most famous human being on earth, should even bother to say hello to an unemployed nobody living in some God-forsaken English town – let alone fork out a fortune on his behalf – for the mere reason of being a fan. The unemployment rate was high, and without a trade there was no work around for unskilled labourers like me. So, in defiance of the doctor's advice a few years back about my health, I sought work, trying building sites, coal yards, factories – but there was nothing. Ultimately I wrote to Muhammad, who was still in Miami, explaining that the Department of Social Security did not believe the truth. I never mentioned any of the other problems I was faced with – namely money and health – and carefully worded my letter to convey the erroneous impression that everything was all right. I posted the letter by express mail. His reply was prompt. It came in the form of a two-page telegram confirming that he had invited me to America personally as his guest and taken care of all expenses. He signed the telegram 'From your friend Muhammad Ali'.

The moment I received this telegram, I took the bus into

Oxford and went to the Social Security Offices. The air was
punctuated with astonished exclamations when I presented
the telegram. It seemed as though all the staff crowded to
look as if examining some kind of rare gem. One jestful
wise-crack was could they keep it and frame it. Anyway,
Muhammad's telegram solved matters and my entitlement to
unemployment benefit was immediately restored. So I continued to live with the embarrassment of having to subsist
from state hand-outs. I had no other option.

By now news of my efforts continued to reach the ears of
many people all over the world, evident by the mail I
received. From Australia, Egypt, Turkey, Libya, Saudi-
Arabia, Brazil, Africa, even from China, they poured in.
This was ironic, because my efforts were ignored by the news
media at the beginning when I most needed their co-
operation, so I assumed that news of those efforts and the
erection of the fan-club got around by word of mouth. I also
began to receive complimentary messages from a few celebrities in England, among them footballers George Best and
Bobby Moore. In due course, and at my request, those two
became Honorary Members of Ali's Fan-Club. I've never
had the pleasure of meeting Bobby Moore, though we've
corresponded and chatted on the telephone; but I met
George Best, whom I really took to, and it was evident that
both were rabid fans of Muhammad. When I went up to
George's ultra-modern home in Manchester, he treated me
with great hospitality and spent most of the time going
on about Muhammad. He and Muhammad had one thing
in common – both were being forever hounded by news-
men. So when, later in the year, George made one of his
mysterious disappearances from the football scene and consequently captured the headlines for quite some time,
Muhammad was, in a sense, 'none-too-happy'. When I rang
him one day to say hello and enquire into his itinerary, he

said, "Tell that George Best to watch it or I'll come over there and sort him out. Ain't nobody supposed to make that kinda noise 'cept Muhammad Ali."

I recorded the message on a cassette and played it over to George on the phone in due course. A couple of days later I received a letter from George, in which he had written a short poem in response to Muhammad's challenge and wanted published in the Fan-Club Newsletter. It read . . .

When Ali says watch it, even when it's for fun
Then either take notice, get help, or just run.

Soon I had to abandon the monthly magazine as a result of the increase in printing costs, and published instead a monthly two-page newsletter. The leaflet consisted of exclusive up-to-date news about Muhammad along with monthly messages from him personally. The fans seemed delighted with my services, and it was nice to receive the constant flow of appreciative letters. But no one knew what problems I was faced with. Still I carried on regardless.

Back on Muhammad's scene, the great man continued to remain active with fights at frequent intervals, outclassing his opponents with the magical skill that the world had come to love. It was his fight against one Alvin Blue Lewis which was of special significance to me. When I talked to Muhammad on the phone after his previous fight to congratulate him on his spectacular win, he said, to my amazement, "Paddy, ah want you to come into the ring with me and be in ma corner for the Lewis fight. Ah'm inviting you to Dublin and ah want you to be with me as my personal guest during my stay in Ireland."

Needless to say, I was thrilled to pieces.

The Opperman Country Club Hotel was several miles outside Dublin, beautifully surrounded by the Wicklow

Mountains. Muhammad had arranged for me to have a luxury suite to myself. At the time there was only one member of his family whom I had not yet had the pleasure of meeting – his younger brother Rahaman. There was a striking resemblance between the two brothers, though Rahaman had their father's dark complexion and somewhat hard features, while Muhammad took after Mama's honey complexion and baby features. Rahaman was as big as Muhammad, though his moustache made him seem huskier somehow. His handshake was firm, his voice warm and sincere. "My brother has told me a lot about you," he said when Muhammad affected the introductions. Ever since that first meeting, I'm proud to say that Rahaman and I have become good friends.

When Muhammad informed the Irish Boxing Board of Control that he wanted me to be with him in his corner for the big fight, it was met with opposition, the reason being that I did not possess a second's licence. In their attempts to change Muhammad's mind, a senior official from the board was sent to see Muhammad and I at our hotel. But Muhammad remained adamant, and the man went away most unhappily. Before long things were hotting up behind the scenes, though the public were not aware of the fuss. Finally, in a last effort to change Muhammad's mind, the secretary of the board came out to the hotel in person. In the presence of a number of people in the suite, he courteously protested to Muhammad that this was just not to be. Not wishing to be the centre of a great row, I expressed my appreciation to Muhammad for his efforts to get me in his corner and explained that I was quite prepared to sacrifice this privilege. A sigh of relief came from the board secretary, with a hint of a smile on his stern face of officialdom. There was a brief but charged silence as Muhammad looked across at me as if weighing up the situation. The silence was broken as the secretary rose to his feet, saying, "Ah well, I'm glad that's all sorted out. You see, it just couldn't be allowed."

To everybody's surprise, Muhammad replied, "Well, it's gonna have to be allowed, 'cause ah want Paddy with me in ma corner and no fussin' about it!"

The secretary left with tongue-in-cheek and we heard no more about the matter until the night before the fight, when news reached us to the effect that the senior officials of the board had given their consent (reluctantly no doubt). Early the next morning, on the day of the big fight, Muhammad handed me what must surely be the most unusual second's licence ever produced. It was made out in my name c/o Muhammad Ali for 'One Show Only'. The Boxing Board of Control had clearly recognised that Muhammad was a very strong-minded person, and once his mind was made up on a matter, that was that: as a result they acted accordingly. All the fuss they had created initially was so unnecessary, since my function in Muhammad's corner was to be nothing more than merely to be there. From my standpoint, of course, to be with him as he entered and left the ring was a great honour.

During the week that we were in Ireland, a large number of people visited the hotel where we were staying to pay their greetings to the great man. They included prominent figures like former MP Bernadette Devlin, film producer John Houston and actor Peter O'Toole. Of all the visitors who called, I notice that Muhammad showed particular interest in Bernadette Devlin, and he invited her and her husband to lunch with us in the hotel restaurant. It is no secret that she is a rabid fan of Muhammad, and was known to have screamed herself hoarse at the ringside when Muhammad first fought Joe Frazier, chanting 'Alee . . . Alee . . . Alee'. She sat next to Muhammad as we lunched, and hardly let anyone else get a word in edgeways. Obviously Muhammad took to her, for he told me afterwards, "Yeah, Paddy, she's a good person; she's honest and sincere."

During our stay in Ireland, there was one major event other than the fight that I cannot resist recounting. I accompanied him on an early-morning drive into Dublin one day to take a look at the outdoor stadium where the fight was to take place. As we drove through the deserted side-streets amid a slight morning mist, Muhammad glimpsed an elderly corporation worker who was limping along as he swept the road. Suddenly Muhammad told the chauffeur to pull up, and next moment struggled out of the large limousine and walked across to talk to the crippled old man. I recall the look of amazement on the old Charlie's face as he dropped his broom to rub both his eyes as if making sure his imagination was not playing tricks on him. He seemed momentarily stunned as he gazed up at the huge frame of the most famous man on earth towering over him. Next instant an expression I read as delight swept over his wrinkled features as he reached out to shake Muhammad's hand and chat with him. Meanwhile I was sitting in the limousine listening to the chauffeur's amazed remarks as well as keeping my eyes fixed on the astonished features of the old road-sweeper. There was a distinct note of ignorance and 'snobbery' in the chauffeur's voice as he said, "I'd have to have seen this to believe it . . .". He named a number of international celebrities to whom he had been assigned in the past, saying, "None of them would even dream of asking me to stop in a little side-street just to talk to anyone, let alone a road-sweeper. I would have thought that Mr Ali would be the last person on earth to do such a thing."

He unwittingly touched a sore spot on me with that remark.

"What made you think that?" I queried.

"Well, he's too rich and famous to talk to low-class people," was the reply.

"If that old road-sweeper were to die tomorrow do you think God would turn his back on him just because he's not rich and famous?" I returned.

This seemed to floor him momentarily. Then he stuttered, "No."

"Then don't you think you have the wrong attitude?" I said.

To this he volunteered no answer, so evidently taken by surprise by the tone of rebuke in my voice.

At that moment Muhammad was saying cheerio to the old man, handing him some money. As they shook hands, the old man seemed totally overcome by emotion.

As the car pulled away, Muhammad said, "Now that was jess a little thing for me to do, but it meant a lot to that old man."

I couldn't resist looking round through the rear window, and as I somehow expected, saw the old man standing alone in the deserted street, waving his cap at us until we turned off out of view. Yes, that consideration on Muhammad's part certainly meant a lot to that old man. It also meant a lot to me.

*   *   *

The big fight atmosphere engulfed everyone with its air of magical excitement. There was so much toing-and-froing around the Muhammad Ali circle, press celebrities, wellwishers, sportsmen, the lot. Nobody would leave Muhammad alone. There were invitations every other hour, up until the day before the fight. One invitation he could

60

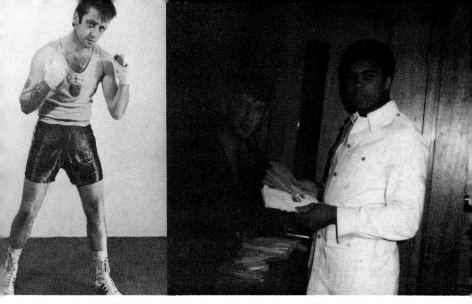

ABOVE LEFT Paddy the boxer. He introduced boxing to Abingdon.

ABOVE RIGHT In Muhammad Ali's London Hotel during Paddy's first meeting with the champ.

BELOW Muhammad and Paddy during the early stages of their friendship. The Champ is reading some of the fan letters from the *Ali Fan Club*, of which Paddy is the president.

ABOVE Paddy accompanying Muhammad at a business meeting in New York.

ABOVE One of the many chat-shows during which Muhammad Ali introduced Paddy to the audience.
BELOW Together in Miami, U.S.A. . . . *Black Crusoe, White Friday.*

ABOVE LEFT Muhammad playing with Paddy's kids.

ABOVE RIGHT Muhammad with Paddy's family in the author's house. Fourth from left is Paddy's mother.

BELOW Paddy and Muhammad Ali outside the Champ's home in Philadelphia, holding *The People's Champion* trophy presented by Paddy on behalf of the fan club.

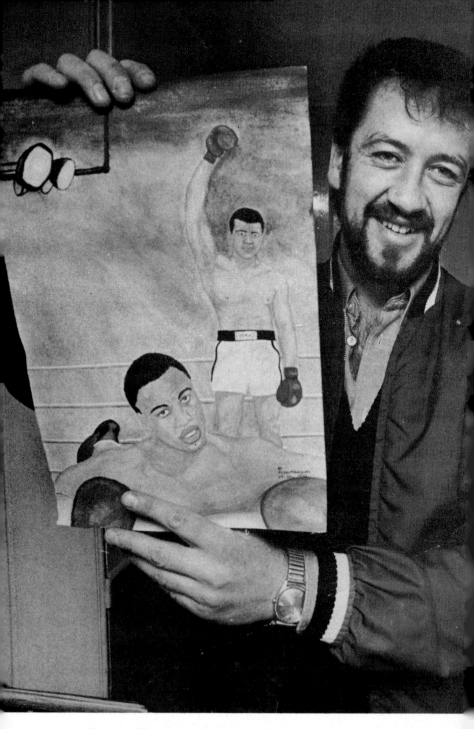

"Paddy–Ali" with his drawing predicting the outcome of the second Ali-Frazier showdown.

ABOVE Muhammad at play. His brother Rahaman looks on right. Paddy is third from left on the porch. The place is in Southern Ireland, where Ali fought Al Blue Lewis.

BELOW Fearsome heavyweight boxer George Foreman (on the back of motorcycle) seconds before his confrontation with Paddy, whose *Ali is our Champ* banner is visible in the background.

Paddy's wife Sandra with their children — all rabid fans of Muhammad Ali.

ABOVE Paddy dining in New York with the family of legendary ex-boxing champion Jack Dempsey.

BELOW The crowd that mobbed Muhammad outside Paddy's home.

ABOVE Muhammad Ali with Paddy shaking hands with local Morris Dancers outside Paddy's home.

BELOW Muhammad Ali with Paddy addressing an impatient crowd outside Paddy's home.

not very well turn down was by Jack Lynch, the then Prime Minister of Ireland. This was the first time that Muhammad received an invitation from a Western Head of State, and he asked me to come along. We met the Prime Minister and members of parliament at his official residence, and Muhammad was given a most enthusiastic welcome. Muhammad's brother Rahaman and two of the Champ's associates were introduced, and during the introduction ritual I remained seated in a quiet corner of the room. I caught a glimpse of the back of Muhammad's head moving from side to side as if he were looking for someone in particular. Then I heard him ask, "Where's Paddy?"

"I'm back here Muhammad," I heard myself say.

Then Rahaman turned and beckoned me over, and Muhammad introduced me to the Irish Head of State.

"Oh yes, Paddy Monaghan," said the Prime Minister as he shook my hand, "I've heard people talk very highly of you; you're quite some character, you know. It's a pleasure to meet you, Paddy."

I thanked the Prime Minister for his compliment.

He and the members of his parliament requested Muhammad's autograph, and were given it. The Prime Minister's parting words to Muhammad were, "Muhammad, I've met some great men in my time but you really are the greatest."

Muhammad smiled (you could almost see him blush!) and lowered his head, pretending to be embarrassed, then replied softly in jest, "Oh, ah knows it."

Mr Lynch wiped the tears of laughter from his eyes. Everybody roared with laughter.

"I'll be cheering for you on the night of the fight," the Prime Minister told Muhammad.

*   *   *

In the dressing-room before the big fight, Muhammad was cool, calm and collected. There was no sign of tension. He laughed and joked and lay back on the rubbing table while the skilled hands of his Spanish-Cuban masseur, himself a tough ex-boxer, toned his muscles, at the same time teaching Muhammad a few more words of Spanish.

Soon it was time for us to leave for the ring, and Luis ended his massaging-cum-Spanish lesson with a playful tap on Muhammad's tummy as he said, "Ah Mantequilla" (smooth as butter). There was a knock on the dressing-room door, and a voice called, "When you're ready Muhammad." Before we left, Muhammad and his hefty manager, Herbert Muhammad, stood side by side in prayer to the Almighty Allah, as they do before and after every fight.

As we headed out to the stadium and into the ring, the roars and cheers for Muhammad sent a deafening echo throughout the open-air stadium. It was a pleasant summer evening and the stadium was bursting at the seams with the crowds. By the time we climbed through the ropes into the huge ring, the stadium was just one endless humming of excitement. But no one could have been more excited than I was. To be the personal guest of Muhammad in the corner was *some* experience. There is nothing quite like witnessing such a grand occasion at such close range – so very different from sitting at home making do with a television set. It was better even than ringside seats; for here you bear witness to the true power of the punches, the skill, the sweat, the real suffering involved.

Soon the two big men were at it. Opponent Al Blue Lewis was a massive black man, as big as Muhammad, American, and a ruthless fighter well known for his punching power. From where I stood, you could see every sweat that flew, you could hear the harsh breathing of the two fighters, you could feel every punch exchanged hit you in the guts with a bang

and a wallop; and as the two men poised, waited, stalked,
feinted, and circled each other, you could almost feel the
feverish working of their brains trying to outwit one another.
But Al Blue Lewis was up against *The Master*. His strength
was no match for the speed and lightning reflexes of the
elusive dancing king who was frustrating him. I need make
no more comparisons. In the fifth round, a short powerful
right-hander from Muhammad seemed to explode on Al
Lewis' jaw. Big Blue keeled over like a giant pine tree. But
Big Blue was tough, he was a fighter, he was no mummy's
pet. As the American referee began the countdown, Big Blue
reached far down into the obscure remnants of ebbing
strength and hauled himself up, and for round after round
the two big men pounded out the issue. The dancing master
continued to tra-la-la out of trouble with cat-like grace and
blinding speed. The crowd meanwhile was in uproar, hollering for Muhammad to finish it.

At the end of the tenth round Muhammad returned to his
corner with his face contorted in agony. As I swung his
corner-stool around the ring-post into position for him, he
slumped down and pressed a begloved hand on to his
'protector-cup', groaning, "Oooohhh, aaaahhh, oh geeee,
ooooohhhh."

Trainer Angelo Dundee anxiously leaped through the
ropes thinking Muhammad had been dealt a low blow.

"What the hell's the matter?" cried Angelo as Muhammad
continued to groan. "Did that motherfucker catch you in the
balls?"

"Naw, my nuts are okay," Muhammad managed, ". . .
ohhhh geeee, ohhhh, ah sure am bursting to have a piss!"

Angelo and I sighed in relief.

"What number's the next round, Angie?" Muhammad
gasped.

"The next is the eleventh," Angelo told him.

"Well, ah guess the crowd's happy enough by now," said Muhammad, "so ah'm jess gonna have to finish him off this next round 'cos ah gotta have a piss!"

Sure enough, he went out and finished Lewis off in the eleventh round.

His main concern after that was to get back to the dressing-room as soon as possible. He made it in the end, and in so doing jested, "If that fight had lasted much longer ah guess everyone would have needed umbrellas!"

*   *   *

As time progressed, Muhammad remained active in boxing, thrashing his opponents out of sight. I always travelled to London to watch his fights live on close-circuit television. After each fight, the famous commentator Reg Gutteridge got into the ring to inverview Muhammad, and the great man would always find room in his memory to say, "Hallo to ma best friend there in London, England – Paddy Monaghan. He's ma main man." Then he'd wink at the camera and add, "Okay, Paddy, call me next week."

I've always regarded it as an honour that he should even think of someone so insignificant as I was after one of his big fights.

By now the amount of fan-mails streaming into my home for Muhammad surpassed anything I could have imagined possible; and of course I would reply to each and every one, regularly sitting up until four or five o'clock in the morning to do so. I would often have a correspondence page in the issues of the fan-club journal, and one such particular letter is worth bringing to the reader's notice. It came from a 'little' Joyce Kitchen in Manchester, and its contents speak for themselves.

Dear Paddy,
  I have just turned 9 on January 17th and would you let me join the Muhammad Ali Fan Club cos I love him. I have got tin legs cos I was in a plane crash, and I have to go back to hospital soon as they hurt me. In July I am going home to Louisville Kentucky. I went to see Muhammad in Stratford. But they wouldn't let me in cos I was in a wheelchair. Will you write to me before I go into hospital please.
  With love from Joyce Kitchen, Age 9 years old.

The fact that she was so young, had the same birthday and was born in the same town as Muhammad somehow contributed to the element of tragedy that had befallen this child. So I felt compelled to give her special attention. I sent her a large life-sized poster of Muhammad along with several photographs, and in the accompanying letter enquired about her family circumstances. She replied that both her parents had died in the plane crash, and she herself was now under the care of a widowed aunt.

I became more determined then ever to do all I could for poor Joyce to bring a little happiness into her life. Regularly I would send her little boxes of sweets and other items which I couldn't really afford. On another occasion, towards Christmas, I bought her a large doll with money which I had saved to get a pullover for myself – after which I had just enough cash left to send it to Manchester, where she lived.

For about six months, I continued to regard Joyce as a deserving cause and someone extra special, until . . . one day the sports editor of the 'Associated Press', Mr Geoffrey

Miller, telephoned me to enquire about the nationalities and types of people who belonged to Muhammad's fan-club. I felt that little Joyce warranted particular mention. Geoffrey Miller was so moved by the tragedies which had befallen this child that he sent a reporter to visit her in Manchester. Then, just a couple of days later, back came the staggering information from Mr Miller to the effect that the 'poor – oh so poor little Joyce Miller' was in fact a perfectly healthy middle-aged woman!

Naturally this news came as a blow at first, and I was furious for having been the victim of an outrageous con-trick: an expensive con-trick, at that. Yet, in an inverted, lunatic way, I was glad to know that little Joyce Kitchen did not exist – at least not in the way which I had been led to believe: for I now know that she is not a child in grief and pain. I wrote off the experience with the observation that she was clearly a sick and frustrated woman obsessed with a craving for attention. Nevertheless, I recognised that she was a well-advanced student of deception.

That experience contributed in helping me to sort out the genuine Ali fans from the cranks. The cranks always told a story of woe and hardship, intimating in a discreet but insistent way that a little money-payment would not come amiss to people in their difficult situations. Providing such letters did not fall into the region of absurdity, I would still pass them on to Muhammad, knowing he would do the right thing in his eyes. There was an abundance of absurd letters, which were promptly relegated to the dustbin. One man in Auckland, New Zealand, for instance, claimed that he had discovered the secret of eternal youth and he would impart this secret to Muhammad for 50,000 dollars! Another fellow, an Asian, claimed to be a good Muslim who prayed regularly, so would Muhammad send him the money to buy a house. Needless to say, a good Muslim would never write such a letter. Muhammad's true fans had only praises and well-wishes for him, with no mention of money.

My friendship with Muhammad meant my becoming the target for so many people in search of money – hangers-on, hustlers and businessmen, big and small, who approached me in order to get a quick route to Muhammad. Over the years I have turned down a great number of monetary offers from these business speculators, and refused to co-operate with them in any way. Basically they wanted me to be their 'contact man', their offers of payment varying considerably in size, large and not-so-large. Although I was flat-broke, my answer was invariably the same – a flat 'No'. Many people have constantly hinted that I was sick in the head for not taking advantage of my opportunities, but I have been singularly unconcerned with these criticisms. First and foremost my friendship with Muhammad was based on sincerity: try to exploit it, and there is no friendship. Secondly, in the case of the long line of business speculators, it was the genuine attitudes which lay behind their facades of charm and affability which strengthened that pre-set resolution not to drag money into my friendship with Muhammad. In their eyes I was really a nobody whose only useful role was as a convenient bridge to good business. I suppose one could forgive them, in a way, sport being, after all, about big money and big people whose sense of values differed so much from my own. When they realised I was not their man, the expression on their faces or in their tones almost made audible their thoughts: "Just who the hell does he think he is? He's a penniless nobody. I'm worth a million of his kind. I've got a Rolls-Royce and all he's got is aching feet and holes in his shoes. I get my clothes from Savile Row, he dresses like someone from Skid Row . . . Ha! He's just a nobody and people like me don't talk to nobodys . . ."

They should have then reflected, "But err . . . er . . .

but . . . I went to him, he never came to me. So, if he's just a nobody then what am I?"

One can only hope that some of those 'big people' will learn that the word *nobody* no longer has a recognisable identity. As soon as we are conceived from our fathers' seeds in our mothers' wombs, then life begins; only without life does the word *nobody* qualify as logic. But in life we all have a purpose, be it great, be it small: no universal code states that any one man has priority over another.

Chapter Five

I published the last consecutive monthly newsletter in March 1973 because I had run out of all the personal items which I had to sell in order to keep the monthly newsletter going: my old car was gone, I'd sold my overcoat, watch, and in due course my film projector and boxing film collection were to go. Since March 1973, I've only been able to produce the newsletters on staggered occasions, yet, to my surprise, there has never been any let-up in the flow of Ali-fan letters into my home. I have often wondered just what the total amount would be of the letters I've replied to since 1967.

However, life as Muhammad's pal continued to bring in other pleasantries aside from fan-letters. I once received a request from a department of the Home Office, from the Chief Liaison Officer Mr Western, to visit Wakefield Maximum Security Prison in Yorkshire as guest speaker. It was a challenge I couldn't resist, in spite of the great distance I was required to travel: many of the fan-letters I had received over the years had come from prisoners in various jails around the country. This was a service which Muhammad would have been keen that I carry out, being a sympathiser of the under-privileged. I borrowed an uninsured car and drove up to Yorkshire, recognising how ironical it would sound if the guest speaker for a prison was caught driving a car without an insurance. I had to use the money I had set aside for the next newsletter to top up the petrol tank after assurance from the liaison officer that I would be refunded travelling expenses.

The recreation hall in the prison was packed; there was not one empty seat. Mr Western introduced me on the stage, and the lads greeted me with enthusiastic cheers and claps. My talk-in lasted two and a half hours, included a film of the second Muhammad Ali–Henry Cooper fight, showed with my soon-to-be-sold projector. I was astonished at the enthusiasm displayed by all the prisoners, and their interest to know more about myself. The ovation after the talk-in would have had to be witnessed to be believed. As I was leaving, many of them formed a large queue around the perimeter of the hall in order to shake by hand in turn. Mr Western expressed surprise at the reception I received, remarking that he had never seen such favourable response from maximum security prisoners towards a guest speaker. For me it had been a pleasure: I would have been prepared to go to hell and back to talk to them, if only for the sake of bringing some happiness to their otherwise wretched existence.

Back on the world scene, Muhammad continued to fight regularly and eliminate all opposition in his campaign to get back the World Heavyweight Championship. A further delay occurred, however, brought about by an amazing event that (pardon the expression) 'buggered' Muhammad's plans. The supposed 'indestructible' Smokin' Joe Frazier was battered to defeat in two rounds by an amazon of a giant called George Foreman, who knocked Frazier down six times in the process, his last blow connecting with such devastation that it literally lifted Frazier clear off the canvas with both feet at the same time! A unique achievement.

Now George Foreman was the new heavyweight champion, and Muhammad had *two* people to contend with – Frazier and Foreman. Now the so-called experts were hollering awesome praises for the new champion. They said he was the most dangerous unarmed man in the world. That was the same thing they said about Sonny Liston before Muhammad demolished him. Now they were saying that Muhammad would be eaten alive by 'Fearsome Foreman'. In the newsletter, I voiced the opinion that Muhammad would one day annihilate Foreman inside the distance, and regain the championship.

Meanwhile Muhammad, unmoved with the glowing critics' testimonials of Foreman, continued to remain the most active heavyweight boxer in the world. Then a very uncanny thing happened. He took on a massive ex-marine Negro from San Diego called Ken Norton. The BBC transmitted the fight live and I watched it on home TV in the company of all my family and a couple of friends.

As we watched the action towards the end of the *second round*, I let out a sharp painful "Oowww! God!" after biting on a boiled sweet. My family and friends attended me anxiously as I removed part of the chipped tooth from my mouth. Later, the world was to learn that Norton broke Muhammad's jaw. What they were not of course to know was that the jaw had been broken at the same time as I felt the sharp pain in my mouth. If this was just a coincidence, I regarded it as a strange one – so much so that I have never mentioned it to anyone before, as it would have sounded too farcical. I've never even told Muhammad about it for that same reason. But now I can write about it, because it is true.

Back to that occasion, when Muhammad came out for the third round, the world was not aware at the time what had happened to him. Yet, though I was six thousand miles away, I could sense that something was badly wrong. Time and time again, as the fight progressed, I kept telling everybody in the room, "Something is wrong with Muhammad. I don't know what it is, but I can feel it in my bones. . ."

The fight was, of course, a non-title bout, scheduled for twelve rounds, and by the end of the last round, it was clear that Muhammad's performance throughout was well below his normal. Nevertheless, when the bell rang to end the fight, I still felt that Muhammad had done enough to win. So did the commentator Harry Carpenter. During the last seconds of the final round, he declared, "Ali has proved himself yet again." But, to my horror, the judges thought differently. The announcement of the result hit me like a douche of ice-cold water. "Laydeeeez an' Gentlemen, the winner, by a split decision, Kenny Norton."

When I heard the news about the broken jaw, the fight result was of secondary importance. My sole concern was for the 'man', not the 'boxer'. I wanted to do something to help boost Muhammad's morale. As far as I was concerned, he didn't need to win fights or regain the championship. Now was the time he would find out just who his true friends were. At the same time, I would prove to him that he was still 'The People's Champion', and always would be. While the world was speculating as to whether the loss now meant the end of his boxing career, I knew all along he would not retire: it wouldn't be like Muhammad to retire on those terms: his pride would goad him into recapturing that crown.

However, I designed a trophy of Muhammad as 'The People's Champion', and took a drawing of the Champ's face to a London craftsman for an estimate on having it engraved on the trophy. The figure he quoted was fifty pounds. I did not have fifty pennies to my name, let alone fifty pounds. When I got home I worked through the night replying to all the day's fan-mail, and, for the first time ever, asked for a donation from the fans to contribute towards this trophy. Every fan to whom I made this appeal responded. There was one in particular who deserves a special mention, a woman

72

called Marina Westwood. She not only contributed and acted as 'treasurer' for 'The People's Trophy Appeal', but also offered to pay for me to travel to America and back in order to personally present the trophy to 'The People's Champ'. I went up to London to collect the trophy, and well recall the hearty congratulations I poured on the craftsman for a first-class piece of work.

So, just a few weeks after the Norton fight, I was off to the States for the presentation. I hoped deeply that this action would reassure Muhammad that he would always receive heartfelt loyalty from all over the world. I also took with me a large suitcase crammed tight with fan-letters. One letter in particular I carried in my breast pocket. It was a letter for Muhammad handed to me by two Oxford University Dons requesting him to become candidate for 'The Professor of Poetry' at Oxford University.

When I arrived at Muhammad's home, I was told, "He's talking business in another part of the house. But make yourself at home, Paddy, he won't be long."

Hoping I wouldn't doze off, I sank myself into one of the deep, comfortable sofas in the living-room. Fortunately I didn't have to fight against sleep, because within what must have been less than five minutes, my nodding head was suddenly gripped in an armlock by two powerful arms from behind; and with this came the unmistakable whisper of a sing-song voice (despite the wired-up jaw) . . . "P-a-a-a-d-e-e-e Monagha-a-an, ma brother."

As we exchanged greetings, I automatically asked him, "How are you feeling?"

He quipped, "Like someone with a broken jaw."

He could only talk through clenched teeth, as his jaws were held together by surgical wires. This meant he could only be fed on soups and other liquid foods. These circumstances would have created an atmosphere of gloom with

73

most men as they nursed the pain of defeat; but not so with Muhammad: I found him as cheerful as ever.

Eventually we got round to talking about the fight. There was no apparent bitterness in his tone. Indeed, he was prepared to alight some of the blame for his 'defeat' on himself for taking Norton too lightly. It was then that he told me that his jaw was broken towards the end of the second round! He said that doctors had told him the jaw was broken by a 'fluke' punch which landed at the precise moment during a split-second relaxation of his jaw. He then jested, "But woulds, coulds, ifs, buts and shoulds don't mean a thing, Paddy, 'cause Norton got the decision, and ah got this . . ." (pointing to his broken jaw). Then he gave me his infamous wink and smile, saying, "But you and ah knows, little brother, that ah'll be back to fight another day."

"I know it, brother," I replied at once.

He jested, "Yeah, man, when ah'm finished with Ken Norton next time, he's just gonna be Ken Nuthin!"

Presently we changed the subject, and he said, "Hey, Paddy, you ain't seen ma son; he's eleven months old now. C'mon and see him."

We joined his family in another living-room and he proudly showed me his baby son Ibn, or Muhammad Jnr. Remarkably it was at that particular moment that Ibn walked for the very first time! More remarkable was the fact that his first steps were towards *me*! – to the exclamations of delight from his parents. He stumbled into my arms. It was almost as if he was awaiting my arrival before he made his first attempts to walk. His first steps have a special meaning for me. This meaning can best be summed up by this short poem by David Hope:

Although we may not understand
The wherefore and the why,

Black Crusoe, White Friday

The first steps we take are those
Which count most by and by —
The truths we learn at our parents knee
Make us the folk we grow up to be.

*   *   *

Over a delicious 'soul food' lunch cooked by Muhammad's wife, I felt a stab of sympathy for Muhammad as he sat at the table looking on longingly as we tucked into the succulent meal, having to be content with sipping his liquids through a straw. I really felt he needed some cheering up after going through this sort of torture, so once dinner was over, I decided to present the trophy to him. I did so in the presence of his family, all sitting in the living-room to let the dinner digest. Muhammad held it in thoughtful silence for some moments, clearly admiring it, then slowly shook his head and said quietly, "Paddy, ah've been awarded so many trophies over all these years that ah've lost count of them all. But, man, this award really means something special to me. Thank you, Paddy, and thank all my fans for me; assure them ah'll treasure this always."

He proudly showed it to his family.

He was also genuinely honoured when I passed on the letter to him requesting him to be candidate for Oxford University's Professor of Poetry. But he said he couldn't accept because of 'this' (and held up the Peoples' Champion Award). He added, "Ah've got to come back to boxing again and whupp Norton and walk tall for all the people."

That same day, he wrote out a polite, appreciative and

75

poetic rejection to the Oxford dons which I was to take back
with me to Britain. It read thus:

> *Pay heed, my children, and you will see,*
> *Why the time is not right for your university.*
> *It's not because of the pay, although it's small,*
> *It's because I have to show the world I can still walk tall.*

On this occasion I spent a week with Muhammad, and
after a couple of quiet days at his home, he invited me to
accompany him on a trip to Canada, where he was to make
his first official public appearance since the Norton fight at a
press conference in Toronto. As we sat at the breakfast table
on the morning that we were to leave for Canada, I noticed
Muhammad giving a lot of attention to something that had
been written on a crumpled piece of old brown paper. When
I finished my breakfast, he passed it across the table to me. It
was unsigned, typed, and in verse. It read:

> *The butterfly has lost his wing*
> *The bee has lost his sting.*
> *You are finished you loud-mouthed braggart*
> *And it's a great day for America.*

Muhammad and I exchanged silent derisory smiles. The
letter was unspokenly dismissed with the contempt it
deserved.

When we arrived in Toronto, the airport was swarming
with well-wishers. Travellers would drop their bags and rush
out to greet him. Many expressed their conviction that he had
been robbed of the decision against Norton. When he predicted the outcome of his return match against Norton with
the words, "Ah'm gonna whupp his ass!", the cheers that
greeted this drowned the sound of jet-engines in the background.

Black Crusoe, White Friday

It was while I was in Toronto with Muhammad that I experienced yet another remarkable incident which portrayed, again, a Muhammad Ali the rest of the world knew nothing about. I accompanied him to some business meeting in the coffee lounge of the plush Sonesta Towers Hotel where we were staying. The two businessmen waiting for Muhammad were puffing impatiently on fat cigars – clearly not the types who appreciated being kept waiting. Both were obese, with the air about them of expensive good tastes that money can buy. When we sat opposite them, I recollect thinking how they reminded me of the characters in *Alice in Wonderland*, Tweedle Dum and Tweedle Dee. However, they talked with Muhammad about some advertising projects as well as other promotional works. But I paid no attention, as the matter did not involve me. I sat there reading through some journals.

Presently a waiter approached us at the table, and courteously enquired if we wanted some more coffee. By so doing, he apparently irritated both businessmen, one of who growled, "Oh fuck off and leave us alone!"

The startled waiter apologised in obvious embarrassment for unwittingly interrupting the conversation. He was about to walk away when Muhammad called him back, and said, "Yes, ah'll have a cup of coffee; and ah want you to take a seat and join me by pouring one out for yourself also. You deserve a break, your job ain't an easy one."

Visibly surprised, the waiter stuttered, "Oh, err . . . but . . . that's very kind of you, Mr Muhammad Ali, sir, but . . . but . . . the management don't allow the staff to sit at the same table and drink with the guests."

"Is that so?" Muhammad answered, then insisted, "No, you gonna join us and drink a cup of coffee at the same table. You tell your boss man that Muhammad Ali says so."

Black Crusoe, White Friday

As the waiter momentarily disappeared, silence stepped in between Muhammad and the businessmen, whose faces simultaneously took on a deep brick-red tinge. They tried to break the silence with embarrassed stutters and stiff attempts to continue the conversation as though the incident had never occurred. But Muhammad totally ignored them and spoke to me.

Presently the waiter returned sporting a broad smile along with a coffee tray, and told Muhammad, "The manager said it was okay."

Muhammad replied in jest, "If he hadn't said it was okay, ah'd have bought this place and he'd a-been looking for a job."

When the waiter sat down beside us he was clearly feeling awkward with 'Tweedle-Dum' and 'Tweedle-Dee' opposite us, but he soon appeared to grow more at ease as Muhammad questioned him with smiling interest about his work in the hotel. The two businessmen now sought to redeem themselves by being polite to the waiter, attempting to get in courteous questions such as, "Yes?. .Oh really?. . .Er. . how long have you worked here then? I bet you're the envy of all your friends right now." But Muhammad would cut them off each time they tried to speak to the waiter, who clearly had no desire to answer them. While all this was happening, the other guests were taking in everything, and one was conscious of the embarrassing tension. Muhammad didn't even bother to touch his coffee, and as we were about to leave, he obligingly gave the delighted waiter his autograph, as requested, and several dollars in tip. After shaking the guy's hand, he said, "C'mon, Paddy, we're going now."

By this time, of course, the two businessmen were speechless, their vocabulary having been reduced to mere grunts, making them sound pathetically like a couple of prehistoric

78

men. Muhammad and I left without saying a word to them, and they remained glued to their seats as though they had all the symptoms of constipation.

Muhammad said nothing more about the incident afterwards. There was really no need to, as the episode spoke for itself.

Chapter Six

In their return match, Muhammad outclassed Norton, and was once more in line to contend for the heavyweight championship. But first he wanted to avenge his defeat by Joe Frazier. Before that happened, however, the official heavyweight champion, George Foreman, was coming for a visit to Britain. When I read this in the newspapers, I felt it was my responsibility to let him know who the real champ was in the eyes of the people. Much as I recognised that I would be laughed off as crazy, I knew that Foreman would not be laughing: my challenge would certainly have some psychological effect on his self-confidence and in his image of himself as true champion. So I didn't give a damn when my pals told me I was round the bend, and headed off to London accompanied only by my large *ALI IS OUR CHAMP* banner. I demonstrated my feelings to George Foreman when he arrived at the Connaught Rooms in Central London to present a Littlewood Pool's winner with a jackpot cheque. I stood outside waiting for him, and when he posed on the back of a motor-cycle, I unrolled the banner and held it high above my head with both hands, standing directly under his nose and blocking his path – just as I did with Frazier a couple of years earlier. Big George – quite a bit bigger even than Muhammad – looked down at me in

81

disbelief then raised his eyes to take in the message on the banner. At first he said nothing – just glared menacingly into my eyes for some moments. I stared back at him, determined to outstare him – which I did. Finally, he gritted his teeth and said, "Motherfucker!" Next moment one of his massive shoulders barged into my face, sending me backwards on unsteady feet. He looked ahead and continued on his unblocked path. The small crowd present took in this 'entertainment' with some amusement.

Although Foreman took my niggling in a much more dignified manner than did Joe Frazier, he was clearly upset and annoyed, though luckily for me he controlled his anger. He and Muhammad just had to face each other some day, and I not only thought Foreman would meet his match, I *knew* it.

Meanwhile the next item on the agenda was Muhammad's return fight with Frazier, which was to take place at Madison Square Garden in New York, and had been designated *Superfight Two*. I would have been contented with just watching the fight live on closed-circuit television. But, to my delight, better was to come. I received a telephone call from the manager of the Dolphin Air Charter Flight Company, requesting a copy of my list of all the addresses of the fan-club members who lived in Britain. In return for my co-operation, I would get a return flight to New York, with free accommodation at the Royal Manhattan Hotel. But he added that he could not provide me with a ticket for the fight. However I knew that once I met Muhammad in New York there would be no problem about my getting in to see the fight. I was over the moon with this golden offer, and sat up into the early hours of the morning writing a copy of my large list of members living in Britain.

Muhammad was staying at some private address in New York, and before I left London, I had no idea where. I left everything until I arrived in New York, where I telephoned his training camp in Pennsylvania; I knew someone was permanently stationed there. I was told that Muhammad was staying at the Royal Essex Hotel. It turned out that it was some of his large entourage staying there. Muhammad himself was staying in a nearby private apartment block overlooking New York's Central Park. It was quite by chance that I happened to bump into his brother Rahaman in the lobby of the Royal Essex, and he promptly took me to Muhammad.

Muhammad was pleasantly surprised to see me, and we exchanged hearty greetings. Present in the room were several members of his entourage, who gave me a collective greeting. When I informed Muhammad that the Air Charter Company could not provide me with a ticket for the fight, he exclaimed, "What! You should know by now that you don't need to rely on any Air Charter Company. You can pick up the phone and call me anytime and ah'll take you anywhere with me to any of ma fights. But you never ask for nuthin'. Anyway, you don't need no ticket, little brother. You've earned that more than you seem to realise, and ah want you to be with me in ma corner when ah fight Frazier."

All I could say was a candid, "Thanks, Muhammad."

As we chatted, he offered to get me a room in the Royal Essex, since he would ultimately be moving in there himself. But I explained that I had already checked into the Royal Manhattan with the rest of the Charter Flight group.

Then he asked, "You okay for bread?"

"I'm okay, thanks Muhammad," I lied.

I left the apartment block and walked back to the Manhattan Hotel, where any meals apart from breakfast had to be paid for as 'extras'. I realised I should have checked into the Essex Hotel as Muhammad had suggested, because I was 'bloody skint' and my stomach was rumbling. So, under-

83

standably, when I got back to my hotel, my first puzzle was
to work out how the hell I was going to eat. I was lounging
around the entrance into the dining-room at the time, and I
noticed that the waitresses were laying the tables, placing
breadrolls in wicker-baskets in the centre of each table.
When the waitresses left the empty dining-room, I nipped in
and stuffed about half a dozen bread-rolls under my open-
necked shirt, and, looking as casual as possible, buttoned up
my jacket in an attempt to conceal my lumpy waistline. I left
the dining-room with tongue-in-cheek and walked across
the lobby, heading for a perfectly placed little recess
positioned in a spot where I could sit unnoticed behind my
newspaper and eat the bread-rolls. At least I thought I was
unnoticed. . . As I put down the newspaper after eating the
last bread-roll, I sat back in the armchair and caught sight of
an elderly but attractive lady standing behind the counter of
a little jewellery foyer in the lobby. She was smiling. She
looked away as I glanced over at her. But her smile aroused
my suspicion that she had spied me stealing the rolls. I
felt a little embarrassed as I walked in her direction, pretending to show interest in her jewellery. There was a hint
of a chuckle in her voice as she asked courteously, "May I
help you, sir?"

When I looked at her and replied, "No, thank you, I'm just
looking," the amusement she was trying disastrously to conceal suddenly surrendered to light-hearted laughter.

"You saw me pinch those rolls, didn't you, ma'am?" I said
with forced courage.

"Yes I did," she confessed, "but don't worry, I won't
report you to the manager." Then she emitted a humorous
gasp, saying, "Why, I've never seen a man with so much
bread before – and I mean that literally!"

She could obviously tell from my accent that I was one of
the group who had flown over from London for the big

fight, for she began to express her love for London, saying how she and her husband had enjoyed their recent visit there.

"Who do you reckon will win the fight?" she asked.

"*Reckon*?!" I exclaimed. "I *know* Muhammad will win." I continued, "Are you interested in boxing, ma'am?" It seemed a silly question to ask a lady, but call it polite conversation.

To my surprise, she answered, "Well I suppose you could say that I have great interest in boxing, yes." She went on to reveal that she had met Muhammad.

Such was my temptation to boast of a similar privilege. But I recognised that if I began to tell her about myself and my past experiences with Muhammad, she would be convinced that my imagination had got the better of me. How could I possibly expect her to believe me? – especially after she had witnessed me steal those rolls? So I said nothing.

The charming lady persisted on the topic of boxing. "Who do you think would have emerged the winner if Muhammad Ali had fought Jack Dempsey at his peak?"

My answer was unwavering. "Ali would have annihilated Dempsey."

At this, the lady placed her fingertips over her lips as if to suppress a shy giggle. I thought nothing of it at first, and at this point I excused myself politely, intending to go up to my room for a good siesta.

But before I could depart, she said, "Oh just a minute . . . I think, after seeing you eat those rolls, that you would appreciate a proper meal, so you are welcome to join my husband and I for dinner if you wish, at my husband's restaurant in Broadway." Her sweet words were like music to my ears. I could hardly believe them.

"Thank you very much, ma'am," I said with respectful candour, "I'd be delighted to; and I sure would appreciate it."

I reached across the counter to shake her hand, and at the same time I introduced myself to her.

"I'm very pleased to meet you, Paddy," she said with that disarming smile, and added, *to my horror*, "I am Mrs Deanna Dempsey – Jack Dempsey's wife!"

I had never felt a bigger idiot in my life after that revelation!

A few hours later I made my way to Jack Dempsey's famous restaurant in Broadway, a mixture of excitement and intrigue churning over inside me. It was well within walking distance from my hotel, and I was so hungry that I could think of nothing else except food. Even as I strolled along Broadway and took in the pumping hips of the enticing 'dolly birds', they reminded me of rump steak – wow! How I yearned to get stuck in.

I arrived at the restaurant at the appointed time, and the place was packed. There was a crowd of people surrounding a table on my left by the door, and through a gap I noticed Mrs Dempsey. I made my way through the crowd to let her know I had arrived.

"Paddy," she said, "glad you came;" and she nodded to a seat for me to join her and a delectable girl who she introduced as her daughter. The crowd lessened, and I caught my first glimpse of her husband – the legendary Jack Dempsey – talking to all and sundry. Mrs Dempsey told me that they themselves had only just arrived, explaining that the crowd always assembled whenever her husband put in an appearance in the restaurant. As I looked at the great old man through the occasional gap in the crowd, his small almond eyes somehow menacingly explained why he had been nick-named *The Manassa Mauler*.

While he chatted with the crowd, I couldn't resist chatting up his daughter at the table. She was in her twenties, with long well-groomed ash-blonde hair framing a pretty and

86

unblemished face untouched by make-up. My attention was momentarily taken away from her by some of the questions her father was answering from his fans.

"Who do you think will win the fight, Jack?"

"Frazier will win," he said; "it has to be Frazier by a knockout."

"Do you think *you* could have beaten Muhammad Ali?"

"Yeah, I could have taken care of him," he reckoned. Then after a hesitation, he went on to praise Muhammad's great service to boxing, but added, "but the guy talks too much!"

I was more interested in the steak that was placed in front of me than the unrealistic fantasies he was spouting. I could have eaten the bloody plate as well I was so famished.

Eventually old Jack Dempsey joined us at the table and we enjoyed a pleasant conversation with our meals. After dinner, the four of us posed for photographs. People kept coming to our table to ask him questions and pose for photos. I got the impression from talking to him that he was the type who believed in the subordinate position of the black man, but I might have been wrong.

When eventually I bade my farewell to the family, I was just reaching the door when I heard him telling the crowd around his table, "Yeah, I could have fixed him; he talks too much." I liked his daughter, and I will be eternally grateful to his delightful wife for having fed me when I was suffering with hunger; but, needless to say, I didn't take to Jack Dempsey. A great fighter though he was, he and I would never have been the best of pals.

Back in my hotel that night, the weather in New York was as cold as an Eskimo's nose, yet this was a sharp contrast to the temperature that filled the air as everybody in this great city awaited the big fight.

I sat with Muhammad in the large limousine that took us

to Madison Square Garden for the fight. There was a massive crowd awaiting Muhammad outside the gigantic stadium, and when a group of them spotted Muhammad in the back seat, they seemed to become uncontrollable with excitement. In no time at all the car was mobbed and the deafening familar chants of "Alee . . . Alee . . . Alee . . ." invaded the atmosphere. Fans climbed on to the bonnet of the car, and for a while I was slightly uneasy. Muhammad opened the window and managed to shake a few hands.

Miraculously the big limousine managed to get through the crowd and parked inside the building. We then made our way to Muhammad's dressing-room, which presently became crammed with celebrities and well-wishers. Among them was young Edward Kennedy Jnr, who had a striking resemblance to his late father President John Kennedy. Edward was accompanied by his glamorous-looking aunt. In the flurry of pleasantries and handshakes, Edward asked Muhammad if after the fight he could be given the trunks which Muhammad wore as a souvenir. Muhammad readily agreed.

Ultimately the dressing-room had to be cleared as the scheduled time drew near. Those who remained were Muhammad's 'boxing camp' and myself. With about ten minutes left before the fight, Muhammad and his brother Rahaman went into the adjoining shower-room to pray to Allah, then rejoined the rest of us. Remarkably, as always, Muhammad was the calmest person in the room. His trainer Angelo Dundee reminded him to watch out for Frazier's head. "You know he uses it as a third weapon, and they let him get away with anything," observed Angelo.

Muhammad nodded, then turned to me and said, "Paddy, you stay close when we get out there, ah don't want you getting lost."

"Will do, Muhammad."

He smiled. "Ah'm dedicating this fight to you, little brother. Ah'm gonna whup Joe Frazier good for putting the muscle on you in London."

Finally a guy knocked at the dressing-room door and announced it was time for us to head for the ring. Bundini, one of Muhammad's training assistants, hollered, "Ooooooeeeeee, lessgo Champ. It's time for war." He was a real clown, Bundini, huge, black, and dangerous if angered, but always an amusing buffoon. He added fun and colour to the camp with his eccentricity.

We made our way down the long corridor. It was lined with policemen, and as we got nearer the entrance, the police cordon was thicker. I stuck close to Muhammad just as he had advised. Then all of a sudden a beefy cop grabbed my shoulder and pulled me back. I called out to Muhammad. I saw him stop and look around. He came stomping back to my aid and through clenched teeth he hollered at the cop, "Take your damned hands off him!" His face was a mask of anger. The big cop released me immediately from the double arm-lock he had applied. Before we continued on our way, Bundini marched back screaming abuse at the cop.

With every step we took we could hear the roars of the crowd growing louder. When we did reach the end of the corridor and walked through the entrance, the atmosphere was electric, the noise of the crowd hitting us like a blast of high voltage. The chants for Muhammad far surpassed those for Frazier.

Frazier was already in the ring when we got there, bouncing and hopping around, looking as menacing as ever. Soon the bell clanged, and the two gladiators were at it. It was boxing at its stirring magical best. It was the artist versus the slugger, the matador versus the bull, brain versus brawn. Muhammad out-fought, out-classed, out-manouevred the bobbing, weaving, bulldozing Joe Frazier, dancing all the way, as if to the sound of his forefathers beating out a special drum-rhythm. He won the fight unanimously, and it was delightful to recognise that such a grand fight had been dedicated to me.

I need not describe the excitement of the crowd afterwards. Suffice it to say that one would have been safer in Vietnam.

The next day I had breakfast with Muhammad and his brother Rahaman, then we were driven to the Felt Forum where Muhammad was to attend an international press conference. I remember that Muhammad was immaculately dressed for the occasion; in his pin-striped suit he looked more like a statesman than a boxer, with his movie-star face totally unmarked after the fight. When we arrived at the Forum, Frazier and his trainer were addressing a packed audience consisting of celebrities and pressmen. Frazier was wearing a hat and a large pair of dark glasses to conceal the bruises and swelling that had totally closed one eye after the fight. He seemed pathetic as he made the usual excuses for losing, claiming he really won the fight and had been robbed of the decision. When Muhammad entered, there was instant pandemonium, the place seemed suddenly to come on fire. Muhammad coolly sat next to Frazier, said hello, and proceeded to dominate the show (as he always does). "Now who was it that said ah was too old?" he hollered at the press. "Who said ah was washed up, ah was finished, and that ah couldn't dance no more? You eat your words, you suckers."

One of the biggest names in British sport who was in New York for the fight was football manager Brian Clough. He was among the multitude of celebrities at the Forum during the press conference, seated with a group of British businessmen. Reg Gutteridge, the *Evening News* boxing correspondent and commentator, was standing just above me, and I heard him whisper in Muhammad's ear, "Muhammad, would you just say Brian Clough's name."

Muhammad turned and replied quietly, "Brian Who? Who's he?"

After further prompting from Gutteridge, Muhammad announced, "We have a Brian Cloof in the audience."

Clough immediately stood up and took a bow.

"Come on up here, Brian," said Muhammad.

Clough made his way on to the stage, and shook hands with Muhammad to pose for all the press photographers. I was to learn that this meeting was played up by the British newspapers to look like the old pals' act, but in reality Muhammad had never seen Brian Clough in his life nor been aware that such a person existed. But of course the British public were not to know that. It was all great publicity for Clough and his business colleagues.

Then, without any prompting whatsoever, Muhammad declared, "Now ah've got someone ah would really like you all to know about. He's someone who has proved that he is a true friend, and ah c'n count ma true friends on the fingers of one hand. I want you all to meet my friend and brother Paddy Monaghan from England. C'mon on up here, Paddy, and let them all see who ah'm talking about."

I climbed up on to the stage and stood by Muhammad's side, and as he continued on his testimonial of my efforts on his behalf over the years. I so wished that Frazier had still been there. He had left not long after Muhammad's entry. All the time he had been there, he kept glancing down at me, as if he had seen my face somewhere before but could not place where. Had he stayed on when Muhammad was introducing me, he surely would have remembered the circumstances in which we met!

When I arrived home in Abingdon, I read all the newspapers' fight reports which Sandra had kept for me. I particularly noted the write-ups of the post-fight press conference. They all devoted a lot of space to the picture of Muhammad meeting Brian Clough, really playing up the 'old-pals' non-sense. Needless to say, not a word was written about the introduction I received. I can't really say it bothered me in the least, to be honest. It was certainly excellent proof of what I stated earlier – that sport is all about big people and big money, and as far as they are concerned, Paddy Monaghan could go to hell. I can only say that if people like them *don't* go to hell, then I'll be happy to go there when my time is up.

Chapter Seven

After Muhammad's classic performance against Frazier, the official champion George Foreman had to remind the world that he was still a force to be reckoned with. He defended his crown against now popular Ken Norton, who was expected by a small number of so-called experts to defeat George Foreman in view of his performance against Muhammad the first time they met. But the general concensus of opinion was for a Foreman victory. They were right. Fearsome Foreman lived up to his nickname by demolishing Norton in the second round with a savagery that was frightening to behold. He knocked Norton down three times into final unconsciousness, with the third knockdown all but ripping off the huge ex-marine's head from his shoulders.

Once again the world press and so-called experts were sounding their ominous warning to Muhammad. But *nobody* alive could defeat Foreman. Many people feared for Muhammad. I managed to save up just about enough money to print another newsletter, and in this I summed up my own views about the impending 'Rumble in the Jungle' – as the fight was designated by Muhammad. I predicted a victory for Muhammad. Of that I was in no doubt.

The fight took place in Kinshasa, Zaire, Central Africa. The world is already aware of the outcome. But for me there are a few glittering fragments of memory that I enjoy to recall during that momentous period. I was just one of the millions who watched the fight on closed-circuit TV. I remember that the crowd's reaction in the cinema after Fearsome Foreman was knocked out was of volcanic proportions. Something resembling a carnival then took place outside. There was a series of strange coincidences that took place *circa* the fight. Muhammad had not only defeated Foreman, but he defeated two of the most powerful representatives of the oppressive system that had taken his crown away – ex-President Nixon and Howard Hughes. Just before the fight, Howard Hughes's health was reported to be seriously on the decline. While at about the same time as the fight, Nixon was rushed to hospital and underwent a three-hour operation as a result of internal bleeding. Could these timely incidents have been some sort of retributive justice? I've often wondered.

Then there was the strange affair about the rains. Weeks before the fight, there had been widespread speculation that the 100,000-seat outdoor stadium might be swamped by a dreadful downpour on the night of the big fight, for Zaire was entering its rainy season. But as the gruelling battle was waged, there was no sight of the rain. Then remarkably, within minutes after the fight, thunder crashed and lightning zig-zagged through the skies as a heavy rainstorm invaded Kinshasa. The stadium was swamped within minutes. It was as if Allah had waited for his beloved son to perform his duty before sending down the rains. It was as if the sound of thunder was the voice of God talking in an international language, with a message that needed no translating. . . . "This here is my beloved son in whom I am well pleased."

I left the dancing ecstatic cinema-goers and returned home to Àbingdon. This was in the early hours of the morning. At that time the only sounds one could usually hear in Abingdon were the birds twittering, the small dogs yapping and the

94

cockerels crowing. But on this occasion, as I walked along
Saxton Road to my council home, curtains moved and bed-
room windows opened as my neighbours leant out to cheer.
They had obviously heard the news about Muhammad's
victory.

As soon as I got into my home, I wasted no time in
expressing my feelings to the world. I pasted four large
posters of Muhammad on the front windows – two upstairs
and two downstairs, and my banner I placed over my front
door.

Within a matter of hours after Muhammad's epic victory, I
was inundated with telegrams from fans from all corners of
earth asking me to extend their congratulations to the great
man. One message simply read, "Hip, hip, hooray!"

*   *   *

At the beginning of December Muhammad breezed into
London for a five-day visit after having returned again to
Zaire as honorary guest for the country's fourteenth independence celebrations. He emerged through Customs at
Heathrow Airport accompanied by his large entourage. His
first reaction came when he sighted me among the large
crowd of assembled well-wishers. He raised his arm high in
the air and loudly called, "Pa-a-a-d-e-e-e Mona-a-a-ghan!
My best friend in England."

He was dressed in a white leather overcoat and carried an
African chief's black ebony walking-stick he received as a gift
from Zaire's President Mobutu. He lifted me off the floor as
we greeted each other, then brushed my chin good-naturedly

with the mighty fist that floored Fearsome Foreman. "Ah was thinking about you, little brother, when ah accepted this invitation to London," he told me. This clearly left the big boxing moguls a bit red-faced. Then Muhammad turned to acknowledge their presence, after which he directed his attention towards me again, and said, "C'mon, little brother, you gonna ride into town with me, and ah want you to be with me throughout ma stay here in England."

I joined him in the chauffeur-driven Rolls-Royce which floated us off towards the Hilton Hotel in London. I couldn't help reflecting on the contrast between this sort of travel and that of yesterday, when I was obliged to walk the seven miles from Abingdon to the unemployment exchange in Oxford because I didn't even have the damned bus fare!

I was given my own plush room at the Hilton Hotel right next to Muhammad's sumptuous suite on the tenth floor – the last place in the world where anybody would expect to find an unemployed labourer. But then my life has been full of surprising twists and windfalls.

In the evening of the first full day of Muhammad's visit, he gave his first ever talk-in show in Europe at the Victoria New Theatre. The theatre was, of course, packed solid. Before he appeared onstage to talk, however, the film of his fight with George Foreman was shown. At the time he had not yet seen the film, and as the light dimmed, about twelve of us sneaked in unnoticed with Muhammad to fill the reserved empty seats in the theatre. So, unknown to the audience, Muhammad himself was sitting in the back row watching the film. I was seated directly in front of him. Throughout the film gasps from the fans in front of us continued to resound – gasps of admiration and love for the great man. "Oh isn't he just gorgeous!" the female voices would exclaim when close-ups of Muhammad's face appeared on the screen. Muhammad would acknowledge each remark with some of

96

his own, followed with a chuckle and a pat on my shoulder. He always disguised his voice when he remarked, "Oh he's just magic!" None of the viewers in front guessed who was spouting these praises. I well remember a particular remark from the viewer directly in front of me. "Cor blimey, Fred," he said, "I 'ope that blooming burk in the back row belts up when Ali comes to talk on stage!"

The actual talk-in itself was an experience many will never forget. It can best be described as a stunning one-man vaudeville.

One of the many places I accompanied Muhammad to was the plush London Sportsman Club, where the great man was invited as guest of honour at a big dinner banquet. It was not really a sportsman's club in the true sense of the word. It was more of a money-mogul's meeting place, with lavishly carpeted floors and elegant crystal chandeliers dangling from the ceiling. It was exclusive only to big businessmen and influential well-to-do figures. The guests there that night seemed very cultured men.

When Muhammad entered the huge clubroom, I recall with sharp clarity the initial 'snubbing' I received by its members. I was a complete stranger to all of them, but that didn't explain the shocked and puzzled expressions on the faces that were fixed at me. I was not to realise until later that the reason was because I had broken the club rule by not wearing a dinner-suit. Not surprisingly I stuck out like a sore thumb.

Muhammad sat in the centre of the top table at the other end of the clubroom with other celebrities like David Frost, Jimmy Hill and Henry Cooper. I sat at a table among a group of well-to-do club members who knew nothing whatsoever about me or who I was – and made no attempt to find out. I did not speak nor was spoken to throughout the meal, which was itself truly splendid. Muhammad satisfied the curiosity

97

of the baffled men during his after-dinner speech. He called me up to the top table and introduced me. He concluded by saying, with a masterful display of tact, that my friendship meant more to him than any other person here tonight, and announced that he was going to honour me by visiting my family in Abingdon. This visit, he said, would be the most sincere part of his stay in England.

After that introduction, the atmosphere in the Sportmen's Club changed dramatically – as did the attitude of everyone present. I received a tremendous ovation, and when I returned to my seat at the back of the hall, everybody was suddenly keen to speak to me. Within seconds they were all coming to the table to greet me, shake hands and ask for my autograph. "Oh, so you're Paddy Monaghan?" was a typical remark. "Heard a lot about you over the years. It's a pleasure to meet you at last." Several people gave me their cards to get in touch. Some of them turned out to be the businessmen I mentioned earlier who wanted to use me as a bridge to get to Muhammad.

The next day I accompanied Muhammad along with his enormous entourage to the Mayfair Theatre, where he was to appear on a special TV screening of the Michael Parkinson chat-show. After it was all over, we made our way out of the building and were heading for the waiting Rolls-Royce when I noticed a breathless Brian Clough, the football manager, ploughing through the crowd behind us. He had been one of the many celebrities in the audience for the Parkinson show. He came running up, calling, "Muhammad . . . Muhammad, please Muhammad, wait just one minute . . ."

Muhammad finally stopped and turned to Clough, who had his two children with him. All he wanted was Muhammad's autograph for them. Hurriedly Muhammad scribbled down the signatures and got into the car without saying a word to Clough: he was impatient to get back to the hotel for

Black Crusoe, White Friday

another important appointment. Clearly Muhammad did not recognise Clough from their brief meeting at the press conference at Madison Square Garden's Felt Forum after the second Frazier fight. As we were seated in the car, I said to Muhammad, "That guy is one of the biggest names in British football."

"Oh yeah, what's his name?" Muhammad enquired.

"Brian Clough," I said.

"Never heard of him," he answered.

I smiled to myself, and didn't think it was worth reminding him that they had met in the States not so long ago: and to think that the British public was under the impression that the two were good old pals!

*   *   *

One of the most memorable occasions in my life was undoubtedly the day that Muhammad came to visit my family and myself in Abingdon. His visit was supposed to be hushed up so that Muhammad could get back to London without any delays that same evening, as he was to make a special appearance at the Royal Albert Hall. But somehow the news leaked out, and on the morning of the day Muhammad came to my home, my wife Sandra phoned me in London to report worriedly that a large excited crowd had congregated outside the house. I told her not to worry and that we would be there as soon as possible, instructing her to call the police if the crowd threatened to get out of hand. In the event she did call the police. But the two constables who turned up came not with any real intention of keeping the crowd in order, but to

99

give Sandra a piece of paper to get Muhammad's signature for them! Sandra was not prepared to say yes or no until she had spoken to me. She was aware of my dislike of the Abingdon police, what with their constant victimisation of the working classes, and because of the mountains they used to make out of molehills when, in my teenage days, they used to get me in court over petty motoring offences and the odd street fights.

"If you agree to do it I'll kick your backside all up Saxton Road," was what I told Sandra when she telephoned again. "Tell them to fuck off."

Being rather on the gentle side, she put it to them more courteously than that, saying that since they had never done anything for us in the past, we would display the same consideration. Don't get me wrong, I know that we can't do without the police force, and I know that not all cops are bad; it's just that here in Abingdon, we don't have any good ones.

Three members of Muhammad's entourage accompanied us to Abingdon. When the car swung into the narrow, drab Saxton Road late that afternoon, we were confronted by an enormously large crowd. They had stopped all traffic, trampled the gardens, and, when Muhammad stepped out of the Rolls, mobbed him and cheered themselves hoarse. Housewives struggled to touch him, one managed to kiss him on the cheek, and screaming boys and girls scrambled to get his autograph. There wasn't one policeman in sight. My mother, who had always been a very sincere fan of his, burst into floods of tears at the thought that he really was here to see us, and kissed him on the cheek. Muhammad appeared quite calm, shaking many of the hands proffered. A couple of Abingdon Morris dancers shook hands and presented him with a set of their dancing bells as souvenirs – normally a presentation bestowed only on Royalty, I later learnt.

At long last we entered my home – to find ourselves

100

accompanied by a few uninvited visitors who had surged in; but they were quickly surged out again. In the lounge of the three-bedroomed council house – whose walls were permanently graced with photos of Muhammad – Sandra served sandwiches and coffee. She was so overwhelmed that it took her several minutes to get her vocal chords in working order. Our fourteen-month-old daughter Belinda bawled her eyes out, and when Muhammad pretended to cry, my other kids sat round howling with laughter. They all gathered round him, taking it in turn to sit on his knee, and really took to him.

Then Muhammad and I went to the door to face the chanting crowd outside. When he raised his hand, a devastating hush fell. Then he said a few words of hello to Abingdon. I took over and informed the crowd that he had a tight schedule and had to get back to London: he had taken time off to come here and do honour to Abingdon. Prompted by shouts of 'Speech' from the crowd, Muhammad began to speak of my loyalty to him, adding that he represented the working class people and the black people of America in their struggle for freedom.

"And from Paddy here from this country, from this town, from this house, came my title *The People's Champion* – a title now known all over the world. As befitting my title, I have taken time to come to this town, to a place I have never heard about. I may never come again, unless Paddy's family invite me. Do you want Paddy to invite me again?"

The affirmative answer from the crowd came in a deafening roar. Then we went back into my house, where he continued to chat with my family.

We were in Abingdon for about an hour. As we were leaving, he handed me a fistful of dollars which he said were for Christmas presents for the children. I passed the money on to Sandra, who was really touched by this kindness.

I accompanied Muhammad back to London, and the next day saw him off at the airport on his way back to America. Exactly a week later, I read in the newspapers that he had accepted an invitation from President Ford to visit the White House. What a contrast to the house and scenery he visited in Saxton Road, Abingdon, a week earlier! I reflected.

I recall that there had been no bevy of local dignitaries to welcome Muhammad when he visited my home. After he returned to the States and I was back with my family, I learnt that there was disappointment in the upper circles of Abingdon at my failure to have invited some of the dignitaries to my home to meet the great man. My response to that was a contemptuous V sign. Except at election times, the working classes did not exist, as far as the local politicians were concerned: so I was happy to return the same attitude when Muhammad visited Abingdon. Besides, it was a private visit.

Be that as it may, with Christmas with us once more, the publicity that my companionship with Muhammad provoked during his visit all but doubled the inflow of fan-mails to my house after he left England. However, not all the Christmas mail I received had greetings to offer. A couple of bigots wrote anti-Irish letters, one of which contained a bomb-threat. This caused some concern to my family, and we notified the police.

"You leave it to us, Mr Monaghan, if any trouble comes we'll be around to clear it up," were the 'charming' words of the sergeant as he left, taking the letter with him.

God bless him!

*   *   *

Black Crusoe, White Friday

The future is what I now await with interest. I have to take life as it comes. My main concern is my family's welfare. My children have never gone hungry; they have always been well-fed and clothed. But because of my work on Muhammad's behalf, Sandra and myself have had to make many sacrifices since April 1967 so that I could continue with my efforts. There have been times when we lived on bread and liquid. In fact, that is pretty well the situation at the time of writing. However, Sandra has always been a great encouragement to me despite the many hardships we've had to suffer. In the meantime, I have continued running the fanclub and pray to God that some opportunity may come my way as a result of what I have done over the years. Remember I was saying earlier about people who reckoned I was sick in the head because I didn't take advantage of my friendship with Muhammad? Well, am I wrong for wanting to eat food that my stomach will accept? – food that I have earned myself? If I am wrong, then excuse me while I go and throw up! As yet there is no happy ending to my story, but if truth comes out in the end, as we are all led to believe, then I'll remain optimistic in my search for truth and a happy ending.